Woman...

RECOGNIZE

GAME ♥

NINE HIGHLY EFFECTIVE WAYS MEN USE TO GET WHAT THEY WANT FROM YOU

AQUARIUS WALKER

SelfPublishMe

DEDICATION

My Lord Jesus Christ

TABLE OF CONTENTS

INTRODUCTION

From a very young adolescent in life, I have always obtained an overwhelming interest in females. The concern was so quelled that it seemed to dominate my thoughts every second of the entire day. Every day, all the way up to this very second, while writing this very sentence!

So, I became a "female addict." From my perspective, I fell deeply in love with talking, listening, hanging around, looking, touching, hugging, squeezing, and receiving all the warmth and unconditional love that God's gift had within her to give to me.

In hindsight, an extremely deceptive thought occurred to me: "If you can get one female to love you, you can arouse an unlimited number of women to love you! That one inkling of a thought influenced me to venture out into the realm of unconstrained possibilities

I am unaware of your addiction, but every species that is currently breathing in oxygen from the earth's atmosphere has one, good or bad. So, you can identify with the term "addict." It is something you need. You maybe unconsciously aware of your addiction or may have mentally brainwashed yourself into thinking that such a thing is obsolete in your life until you are under water too long and your adrenaline kicks in to remind you to rush to the surface to receive and satisfy your "addiction" to air!

Air, to the human race, is a perfect analogy of having the love of a female to me. What would you do if "air" wasn't free and you could not afford it? You would definitely tap into the creative right side of your brain and come up with multiple solutions to solve that problem, no matter what! (well, in some people's circumstances.)

So, identifying the females need of her type of man, I saw there was a way to simultaneously exchange needs by way of camouflaged deception. Basically, I would become whatever she wanted in order to get what I wanted.

During my intense, observational experiences, I began to notice each individual obtained different love to offer for a certain percentage of "the perks" that I was willing to provide. Some negotiated a win/win, some a win/lose, and some a lose/lose philosophy.

Over the years I have evolved into the perfect, complete, whole, "one-woman man." I have paid my dues for deceiving and misleading and hurting many women.

I owe my evolution to every woman that has taught me how to be a "real man." So, I decided to break down every technique I have used to get what I wanted from women. Also forewarn you, and to prevent you from experiencing the mental, emotional, and physical heart breaks that the "female addict" will use to manipulate you into getting what he wants from you!

Chapter One

THE SMOOTH TALKER

M ost lady friends I have paid close attention to, shaved their legs daily. At one point, during their lifespan, everyone came to a conclusion that the protrusions of hair follicles were overwhelmingly irritating. Rough legs generally make them feel unfeminine. They realized, with unshaven, prickly legs, that their inner energy level of sexiness wouldn't extrude the buoyancy experienced previously.

In the Webster's dictionary, the veracity of the word "smooth" states: "Not irregular. To make less difficult." The minutia used above describing the distinct women who loves freshly shaved legs is symbolic to how they cherish a smooth conversationalist man. "The female vs. the smooth talkers" ultra-magnetic enamors attraction is so gargantuan that it would seem he has her in a state of hypnosis!

This person can be described perfectly as a "genteel gentleman." he is very refined, well-bred, elegant, polite, and stylish. He displays noble character, extremely courteous, and maintains a high social position. As a child, he may have been raised in a humongous family dominated by women. From being around his mother, sisters, aunts, female cousins, and all of their friends, he was unconsciously being molded and sculpted into the women's version of the late 80's classic motion feature film called: "Weird Science."

This individual's memory has been loaded with a substantial amount of data concerning the likes and dislikes of women his age, all the way up to two generations his junior! This particular person's keen insights on women became terminally palpable. His "mental sponge" is not dormant like so many men today in this age. There is a saying that states: "Teach a child in the way he should go, and he will not depart from it!" Go figure!

Just ponder all the dissimilar tastes and thought processes "the smooth talker" has digested, analyzed, and cultivated over the years. One person explained to him the uncomfortable scenario of being linked in conversation with someone who only talks about himself. Another methodically exposes the queasiness she feels while listening to an abrupt and vulgar person. The differences range from the tone of voice, topic selection, vast knowledge, interest, and choice words picked to carry on an ongoing conversation.

No one likes a fraud, fake or a phony in any aspect. Consider taking a quick inventory of your close friendships, associates, and yourself. Now locate the gossipers, and people who just unleash the most frivolous syllables known to mankind! I mean, they talk, talk, talk, and keep talking about absolutely nothing! How annoying you may think. Take the same tenacity of the talkative woman and transfer that into *"The Smooth Talker."* Just erase the frivolity and add in the listening part. Love would be an understatement defining how much he likes to listen and converse with the opposite sex. Trust me when I tell you this, this guy is 100% genuine at this. Your instincts will feel it and sense it. Your mind will know it. remember, his addiction is you and this is a highly effective tactic used to feel his and "your" addiction.

Oh! Were you unconsciously unaware that you were an "addict" also? Of course, you are! If you are attracted to this person, you are feeding your addiction of being listened to and understood. Sweetheart, I am sorry, but this thing goes hand in hand. Here is a perfect analogy: " the crack distributor is also addicted to the crack purchaser. Even though they are on two different hemispheres, crack is what they have in common.

The crack is the nucleus and the central core where other elements gather around. Another archetype would be, the manicurist and the pedicurist. You need your nails and feet done and they need someone's feet and nails to do. Money is of no importance to you. Your objective is the services rendered. On the other hand, the services given by the manicurist can be exchanged for some currency. (Are you catching the image I am portraying to you?) they acquire the knowledge, perfection, and expertise you are looking for. "Service" becomes the common denominator.

Wouldn't it be just terrific to come across a guy who paid close attention to small details? Well, that is another aspect that this person has down packed! I would like to label him a "masculine perfectionist metro sexual." He loves the grooming department. From his hair being perfectly cut and trimmed, to his eyebrows being brushed, ears and nose hairs cut, pedicures, manicures, mud mask, apricot scrubs, massages, lotions, and many different scents of colognes, to name a few.

So, if he goes all out for his own personal preferences, he will mental notice anything good about you that reminds him of himself. Then he will verbally give you lavish compliments because he genuinely appreciates the time and energy you took to make yourself presentable. he will make certain inquires, concerning your hair stylist, names of the brands of selected to buy and will even have the foreknowledge to make a couple suggestions for you to test our and broaden your horizons. He will even be a perfect gentleman and surprise you with the gifts!

Can you imagine the longevity of the conversation? You may not expect to miss your favorite television show, or put off our normal shower routine, but you did! Being engaged in such a smooth conversation with this guy will make you feel like you are the only actress on stage of a world-renowned Broadway show! And you have his undivided attention. It wouldn't matter if you were at home in your bed and he was on the other side of the globe, He will still make you feel that way. The monthly order of the priorities you pay your bills are subject to change, also. The electric bill and the water bill will take a backseat to the #1 phone bill!

Obviously, this book is on identifying game, trick ology, and deception, so I will drop you some of the wants he is going to eventually as for in a very subtle way.

While noticing all of your changes to your physicality's, he was simultaneously adding and subtracting your total gross income without directly or indirectly making it apparent. To see if his request would be a financial burden to you or not. He has the knowledge of an auditor and a tax consultant. he just simply uses his business savvy on you! I would like to call him a walking "Non-Profit" organization. He will ask for a donation.

After you have spilled all for your information out and have totally exhausted yourself, it is only natural for you to become the interviewer because he has you interest in the palm of his hands. This is where it becomes extremely interesting. You spoke the truth and guess what? so will he. Up to this point, he knows he has you, but the fish isn't scaled and deboned and fillet over and open fire and placed on a plate, yet.

It's in a women's nature to "nurture." This smooth talker is highly trained to bring that quality out of you and to the forefront. When your questions finally touch his financial situation, he will become brutally honest! All his bills will be paid, except the one, or the tow he needs you to pay for him. (Accordance to your financial situation.) Also, he will drop hints like: " I work a so and so, and it just pays just enough to pay my bills, but my wants are never met. Being that you are taking a considerable amount of interest in this fella, and that you are in a position to lend a helping hand, only the mean woman would not do the judicious thing.

*For a more in depth, insight on how *"The smooth talker"* operates, please allow me to give you a personal illustration....

My girlfriend, a friendly couple and I decided to take a trip to Dallas, Texas. After arriving there we all decided to pull in somewhere and get a bite to eat. Since I was driving, I saw a restaurant that triggered my interest. The place was called: "Taco Cabana." It looked pleasant and inviting. Also, at this point and time, Oklahoma did not have one, yet.

The four of us walker in, I suggested that they have a seat and that I would be a gentleman and order for us all....

Out of my peripheral vision, while standing at the counter, an attractive, green eyed, tanned, jet black hair, 5 feet 8 inches, 140 pound, 36-26-46, Puerto Rican, came walking in all by herself. At 10:30 pm, it seemed odd to me that this attractive lady was alone.

I approached her and said, "Please, allow me to pay for your dinner." Immediately, I told the cashier to add her bill to mine.

I knew immediately that strategic move placed me in a perfect position to checkmate her. More than likely, you are probably wondering, "Where is his girlfriend during all of this?" Yes, I used to be a dog. As a matter of fact, I used to be a pit-bull, and to satisfy your curiosity, my girl was at the table steaming hot! I kept glancing back at her. Plus, to be frank, she knew I was a player, but could not break the stronghold of "game" that I was putting on her.

The Puerto Rican's response was, "Thank you." I asked her name and she replied, "Jessica." Next, I inquired where was she from, and what did she do for a living. In verbatim, I said, "Baby, you must be a model, right? (If she wasn't a model, she sure should have been!)

Jessica's facial expression lit up with a shocking, surprising, and thankful look. Her next words were, "Thank you and you are so sweet. Yes, I am a model, but only part time. But do I really look like one? (Pause....Do you see the garage door of her mind opening wide for me to enter and feed her the flattering reassurance she was so desperately seeking? If I continue to press toward this route, quickly with a smooth finesse, whatever I wanted, she will gladly give it.) My reply was, "Without a doubt!" You can tell from your unique, distinct, facial features, your height, and your posture." Jessica, you are extremely beautiful." (My role in that brief play was executed with precision! All I have to do now is past the questions that she will ask in a moment," I thought to myself.)

Jessica said, "Oh, thank you! It is a career I am seeking, but at the moment I am dancing at a gentlemen's club." (Damn! In my head I am thinking. JACKPOT!!!) My curiosity just peaked at an all-time high!

This is my first encounter with a stripper. Before I could inquire more information, the food came.

Jessica told the cashier that her order was to go. Next, she noticed all the food on the tray and said, "That is a lot of food! You cannot possibly be eating all that by yourself." (Damn! I thought immediately. An obstacle that needed hurdled.) I replied, "Nah, I am here from Oklahoma City just kicking it with a few people."

She looked over the restaurant and spotted my company way at the back. So quickly, I paid the cashier and told Jessica to hold on while I serve my company and be a gentleman and walk her out to her car. I am weaving through the tables, staring at this scrumptious entree thinking to myself, "Damn, I am starving, and I am super busted! Oh well, might as well go all the way!" I sat the tray down and looked at my girlfriend and said, "I will be back." Her eyes fiery engine red with indignation. My girlfriend's friend is in a state of bewilderment, also! My so-called friend is just sitting there like, "Damn! I wish I had all that nerve!"

Ten seconds flew by and I am now accompanying Jessica out her car. She opened the car door, leaned in and bent over in some short, short, short gym shorts to put her food in the passenger's seat and retrieved a book.

Here I am, standing outside the jarred car door, looking at this tight ass, thinking to myself: "Is this girl making a pass at me?" Jessica comes up to her regular height and says: "Would you like to look at my modeling portfolio? I said: "Of course."

By this time, I have shifted my game into 6th gear. I mean, I am hearty in my approbation and lavish in my praise. Her photos were extremely gorgeous!

So, I said: "Where were these taken?" Her reply was "Oh, Albuquerque, New Mexico. That's where I am from." Then I said: "Well, it has definitely been my pleasure meeting and conversing with you. Do you have a telephone number where I can contact you?" She replied: "Yes, I am staying at the Round Tree Hotel. My number is *****️ I am actually just getting off of work. Would you like to come over tonight and keep me company? Just call before you arrive so that I can alert the front desk clerk. They close all doors from 10:30 pm to 6 pm."

If you are smarter than a kindergartener, you can take a guess at my answer. This was just an illustration of the smooth talker's conversation that leads to the end result. So, please forgive me for not satisfying your curiosity on did I or how did I follow up on the task at hand.

I tilt my hat to you and every other woman who reads this book. You are very aware of your need to increase knowledge in order to shorten your borders, concerning men and their scandalous ways. Basically, this information is provided to you to tack on many more layers to your intuition. Knowledge is a two-sided coin. What you don't know could eventually hurt you, and what you do know could protect you.

Some "Smooth Talkers" may not need your money. The situation varies from attention, intellectual stimulation, a backup plan, a place to live, sex, a co-signer, a friend, boredom, or from getting the satisfaction of sharpening his game. The master code in decoding this smooth talker is by finding out the motives behind this person. Therein lies the key.

So, my dear friend, be wise, study, and meditate on this chapter to show yourself approved and ...RECOGNIZE GAME!!!

Chapter Two

THE HUMOROUS PLAYER MASTERY

This particular individual is like by many women. He may be lacking in many aspects of the smooth talker but obtains a quality that is jovial. women are drawn to him because he will brighten up their day and will ease their stress and tension levels. He is charming, sweet, and lovable. He is thoughtful and compassionate enough to manufacture and maneuver in a good joke to make you feel good. Overall, his personality traits, come off to be humble and joyful.

Basically, that sums up the optimistic point of view, but we both know that there is more to the story than meets the eye.....

Say for instance, the Russians and the Chinese wanted to attack the United States U.N. launch different variations of missiles at them. There is one possible way in order for them to carry out their task. That would be to decode and shut down the United States Missile Defense System.

This day and age, women remind me of the U.S. They are strong willed, wise, knowledgeable, and exceedingly powerful. Not to mention, women who have been attacked, and wounded in battle before, (whether mentally or emotionally) are extremely cautious! Their shield of armor is impeccable.

This "Humorous Player Mastery" tosses up an overwhelmingly

deceptive illusion that comes off as unthreatening, and harmless. Hardly any woman takes him seriously. Simultaneously, and unconsciously contemplating on being serious towards him! No, that is a paradoxical illustration!

Why? Why? And I do mean, why do women totally ignore their intuition and pursue the exact thing they are desperately trying to avoid? If a person pitches a 1 % not serious energy ball at you, why even swing?

As a matter of fact, why even go to the game, suit up, and participate? The guy is NOT serious! I may have an idea. Maybe women cannot see at all? I don't know.

I look at this guy as a spy. His Mastery snuck through your guards, sergeants, lieutenants, and every surveillance system protecting your "headquarters." Then he became face to face with you, disguised as part of your army, and conjured up a clever, and spontaneous joke. He knew if he'd just get past all the horse manure and get to speak to the president of your mind and body, he'd be able to trigger that chemical in our brain called "endorphins!"

This type of woman this is attracted to this guy is so easy to spot. Her head will be looking down, shoulders hunched, face all sad and blue, along with a tortoise slow paced walk.

Both descriptions illustrated about their body language and facial expressions sends a signal up high in the sky, like batman does, saying to "the humorous player", Please! Someone brightens up my day! I will be totally appreciative and will give you whatever it is that you want!

This unique guy is very capricious to a woman who doesn't know his caliber. Humor to him inside of his brain, has sort of an evil twist, but does no physical harm.

As soon as he acknowledges the desperate distress signal sent up in the air by the woman, in his head he is automatically projected himself into his idea of a motion feature film that's about to be recorded by a director as soon as he says: "Action, Take one!"

The humorous player is the only actor. The woman of his objective isn't aware of the imagined cameras and production casts. To the guy, he got the job, due to his professionalism, and perfection. So, he has no time for the take #1's, 2's, and 3's. He has to nail this scene now on take #1, or it will tarnish his image of himself!

Yes, he loves the fame, attention, money, and the acting, and he doesn't want to waste the cast time or their budget. More the less, he loathes being a failure and he is his own worst critic. Not Siskel and Ebert. So, he understands the importance of this major role. (Even though it is seriously imagined.)

He has rehearsed this scene several times before. He prepared himself with the self-proclaimed inside joke: "dun, dun, dun, dun, dun! (mental images of tearing his blue buttoned up polo dress shirt open and revealing a black t shirt with the initials "H.P." written in red.) Then he says to himself out loud, she needs a dose of "The Humorous Player!!!" Immediately rushes toward the women while riding on the back of an ostrich! (Image that)

To him, this is his pregame warm up to get himself to laugh. Therefore, when he is in action, it'll be easier to satisfy his opponent. Sounds a little bit silly? huh. Well, it is and so is he! Do you remember or recall that old saying, "If it isn't broke, don't fix it?" Well, you may not be into this type of guy, but who's to say that his mastery is ineffective? What you consciously or unconsciously set yourself up for doesn't mean the next woman does the same.

I'll be more than happy to oblige you in describing an episode I once starred in called, "The Humorous Player strikes back!" (Sounds a little different than the former clarification, huh?)

This fastidious scenario totally took me by surprise. Usually, I am the proactive HP in action, but I birthed the internet of an HP amateur...Ladies edition.

Norman, Oklahoma was the exact city and state the attack took place. I was 16 years old at the time. Early on that evening, at approximately 6pm, me and my partner Jay made previous arrangements on going out. He had the car, and I was his influencer in the entertainment field.

My female friend dropped me off at his parents' house in a purple cavalier. Before I stepped out of her vehicle, I turned to my left (since I was in the passenger's seat) and faced the young, 5 ft 10 inch, sky blue colored eyed, milky faced, 150 pound, double D, busty blonde amazon, and said," Put the car in park, bend over, pull you pants down and slide you panties to one side so I can give them pretty, sexy glutes a kiss goodbye, baby." Of course, she laughed. Who wouldn't? I had to hit her off with one more laugh to pay her for the good deeds she has done by giving me a ride. So, I opened the car door and stepped out toward Jay's silver, two door, 1986 Honda hatchback.

I admit we were both dressed to impress. I was more shocked at how well I trained and influenced my protege's choice select of attire. Jay was wearing a red, two buttoned pullover shirt by Tommy Hilfiger (before we knew..lol) tucked in some solid black brand x Girbauds, with some matching red and black Nike cross trainers. Quite spiffy I might add.

Since I have always been a barber, I cut his hair quite precisely. He had little bitty waves on top of his head, so I gave him what we black folks call a bald fade. (Just in case you are from a different race and unfamiliar with this term)

On the other hand, the student never precedes the teacher. I am wearing some beige polo Khakis, brown polo boots, a brown and leather polo belt, a white cashmere sweater with a big red, white, and blue teddy bear printed on the front. I am also sporting a beige fitted polo hat with a blue polo emblem on the front, white polo t shirt underneath, plaid polo boxers, white polo socks, and some polo sport cologne.

Not only a young 16-year-old wearing over a thousand dollars' worth of clothes, but I felt like a million bucks! And the polo hat was just for show. I had no intentions to wear it. It would have defeated my whole entire purpose of going out.

Since you are a woman please allow me to paint this picture for you. Imagine a guy with long shoulder length hair. Now, picture that same guy with his hair cut very low everywhere except a 50-cent piece size at the top and smack dead in the center of his head! Now, visualize that small piece of long hair divided in two separate braided pig tails with each braid falling to separate sides, and hanging just below the ears. (Are you laughing yet?) Well add to the end of each braid a red, white, and blue butterfly beret that is matching the teddy bear on the sweater!

If I swung my head to the left or the right, it'll look a helicopter propeller trying to start up! That was my entire point. I only wanted to look humorously fine! I wanted to be a good-looking walking joke. Plus, I wanted to catch a female of my standards during the process.

From Del City, Oklahoma to Norman, Oklahoma, the drive takes approximately 30 minutes. The city of Norman is where the University of Oklahoma Sooners football is located. It is basically a college town located at the corner, adjacent from the football stadium is where the destination lies. A small eatery/game-room/club all joined together like a pot of seafood gumbo caters to the young people to middle aged people.

The place was called "Campus Corner." As soon as you enter the establishment, you get the feeling of, "I'll get lucky tonight!" circulating through your entire body.

To the left is a four-booth sitting area and next to that is a counter with ten or so bar stools surrounding a gargantuan open grill where you can see the fat cook prepare your food.

On the right side of the establishment, there is a big jukebox playing loud rambunctious music and nice size dance floor.

As soon as me and Jay stepped foot inside of the place, we were both flabbergasted by the scenery of the gorgeous women, all other entertainment along with the food. We arrived at 7:30 pm, and the place was semi-packed. So, I am standing there looking cocky and arrogant and starts strutting towards the arcade games to loosen up a little bit by playing Galaga. (My all-time favorite.)

Here is where the real game begins, all my short years of life every time I spotted a Galaga machine I began to get tunnel vision. I have always come close to getting a high score, but never did! This time I know I will.

So, I am all in this game and my propellers are propelling all around my head. From behind me, out of nowhere, this drop dead, sexy, gorgeous, young, hot, and sizzling diamond eyed, five-foot-six, 135 pound, 34-24-36 double D breast, tanned, blonde wearing all polo comes within four inches of my ear and screams, "Ha! Ha! Look at his hair!" Totally scaring the living daylights out of me and killing my hopes of beating the high score! That really pissed me off!

She just awakened the angry humorous player! Even though she did it as a means of getting my attention and as a form of letting me know that she loved my flamboyancy. I was still going to hit her with some nasty humor.

Yes, she was the exact female I was looking for, and to me back then a dime a dozen. My arrogant attitude looked at her as a sacrifice. I turned around, scrunched up my eyebrows, and said, "Bitch! Look at your unprofessional bleached blonde hair. Ha! Ha! Ha!" I then walked off in search for another good-looking woman where I could be myself again.

Wouldn't you know that this girl and her friend chased me and Jay down to the ground five minutes later? Yep! She apologized, introduced herself and her friend, gave me her telephone number, and asked me to go out with her the next night!

Boom! That is what I used to call: "The Humorous Player Mastery!" I won't tell you what happened afterward, but just know that my request was her desire.

Finally, my advice to you my dear lady friends is to be alert and extremely cautious. This tactic is highly effective. Figure out his motives and intentions before you drown. Many women fell into the ocean screaming for a life preserver only to have found themselves with a broken heart. So, be wise and... RECOGNIZE GAME!

Chapter Three

THE EXPERIENCED ROMANTIC SCHEME

Are you the type of woman that likes romantic movies or romance novels? Well, I guarantee you that this type of character will make you feel like you are in a movie.

You couldn't even fathom the type of adventures this person will come up with. These types of inventions require a lot of thought, time, energy, and money.

The difference between this guy, the smooth talker, and the humorous player is that he doesn't crack jokes or talks you out of anything. He creates the action! You can call him, "Action Jackson." His whole point is to sweep you off your feet, show you something new, and to blow your mind off your shoulders.

He is exceedingly thoughtful, nice, sweet, empathetic, caring, huggable, and lovable. He has observed this age as being dull and he is also aware that his scheme is very old fashioned, but it works. The only problem that he used to have was identifying and choosing the receptive women. After getting played out of his time frequently by time wasters, he has learned to pick you out of thousand ladies.

You have been courted by the domestic flowers and boring things of that nature, but that is more of a "I am sorry flower" to get you to forgive one of the multiple trespasses.

There is an overwhelming difference between trying to keep you and trying to get you! Then there is him and he combines the two. His objective is to get you and keep you simultaneously. He exercises double thoughts and applies triple the energy.

Think, when was the last time you went out on a date and the guy brought you any type of gift? When was the last time a guy opened your door, or any door for that matter? Or has scooted your chair out for you at a restaurant?

Well, to him, those are the fundamentals necessary to warm you up. To him it is considered "The appetizer," just a little something to carry you over until the main course arrives.

You see it is quite possible to figure a woman out by looking at what she chooses to eat. Most women order a light chef's salad or something close to that nature. Mr. Romantic selects a more extravagant entree that suits his taste. Automatically, the woman's mouth will water, and her mind will start to think, "Dang! I should have ordered what he did because it sure does look tasty."

Many females pretend like they know what they want when in all actuality if you haven't explored different cities, states, countries, galleries, malls, cars, dresses, or etc....how could one really be certain that what they like is really the best? Most quizzes or test questions have a multiple-choice method. All of them sound good, but there is only one that is correct. Mr. Romantic is clearly aware of this.

This individual is equivalent to Richard Gere in the movie "Pretty Woman." Your part in the script is Julia Roberts. They are like night and day and the one that is in the dark (you!) can always see the light. Yes, it is different, and you will feel uncomfortably nervous, but the magnetic pull of attraction is unbearable.

Have you ever heard of the term, "passive aggressive?" Just in case you haven't, it is where a person shows an unharmful action in an aggressive way. My experience is what I would like to call "A lovable fantasy fairytale aggressive."

I can pretty much well guess that once upon a time you have identified with the woman in a movie who at the end finally gets her man. Better yet you have felt a great deal of longing for the woman who luckily gets the charming gentleman.

I admit, during my younger days, I brought the life to the party. As a matter of fact, I was the party! Besides my witty humor and charisma, I toted Mr. 24 pack Budweiser, Ms. Cognac, and Mr. Quarter sack of Mary Jane with me.

Recently, my finances were at an all-time low, and it has been a week since I partied. Basically, I was trying to break bad habits, be a mature young man, and live a more civilized lifestyle.

So, I sit down on the passenger's side of my ride and starts to think, "I sure wish I had a roach of a joint at least to calm my nerves!" I began searching the car vigorously for a roach. As much smoking I had done in this car. I know that I accidentally slipped up somewhere, but I used to be extremely careful knowing that I had gotten pulled over by the police and this car reeked of marijuana. I would go straight to jail So, I frequently hit the car washes seven to ten times a day to get rid of the smell, and to make sure there wasn't any dirt on my pearly white car.

I am getting aggravated with myself for being so damn neat, careful, organized and tidy! It is 15 minutes until 8 and I must get to work, but I need to get high first.

Bam! Underneath the floor mat on the driver's side of the car, was three small, tiny roaches the size of a ladybug. I began to think to myself, "Aquarius, you were slipping man! And you were a weed junkie! You could've left bigger roaches than these!"

I pull out my Mazda manual from the glove box and places it on my lap. I unroll the three ladybug sized roaches. Now I am looking for something to roll this dust in. I don't have any zig zags or the time to go get any. I am so anxious to smoke that my vision caught a glimpse of a torn receipt laying in the open glove box. After quick reasoning, I say to myself, "Oh, what the hell!" I immediately began tearing the receipt and shaping it into a zig zag. I rolled the weed up, lit it and took a toke.

Immediately, I relax, started the engine, and rode off smoking. I pulled up to the stop light before turning in to go to work. I am high as the sky and sitting there with my loud music playing "Easy Lover" by

Phil Collins.

Suddenly, a feeling of paranoia illuminated my mind. I fight through all the fear and pulled into the telemarketing parking lot. I rolled through at least 30 women real slow. Their necks and eyes following and checking to see who I am.

It is 8:01 am on the dot! I parked the car, hop out, hit the car alarm, and began strutting 25 ft. across the parking lot like I was John Travolta in Saturday night fever.

As soon as I walked in, I spotted Lynn looking mighty fine. She says, "Hi Aquarius." Let me walk you around so you can check the place out. I am thinking, "Hell no! I don't want you hanging all over me cramping my style," but I said, "okay."

Everyone was seated on terminals sort of like mini booths. The room was filled with a lot of talking and typing. Women were peeking over their booths stealing glances at me. I am trying to avoid everyone at this point, due to my bloodshot red eyes.

I finally 52 shake Lynn and went to check in with the shift supervisor. I punched in the clock, and the woman handed me four sheets of paper full of paragraphs describing different tactics on how to sell health insurance. I may have been high, but it seemed like a scam because we were targeting the 65-year old's all the way up to the dead. the supervisor then told me to pick any booth I wanted, log on, and then just to follow the script. Just like that!

While walking through this humongous room, I saw an unoccupied booth clear at the back and in the corner. Finally, I sit down and takes a deep breath.

I thought I picked a booth without a neighbor, but my peripheral picked up a woman coming toward my way. She sat exactly right next to me. I scooted my chair all the way up in the booth and tried burying myself in the health care scam. I didn't want anyone to see that I was high.

The woman kept scooting her chair back and trying to be nosy and to look at me. When I wasn't on the phone lying to a customer concerning this health care, she tried to speak. I would type real heavy and quickly on the keyboard, and I would also act if I was in a conversation with someone who was ready to bite for the scam.

Then they hollered, "Break time!" that was when she leapt to the chance to speak. She said, "Excuse me, I am Stephanie. You do know that we have a 45-minute break, don't you?" Finally, I make eye contact with her. I smiled really big and said, "No but thank you for telling me."

Her mouth gaped wide open. Then she bent down inches from my face and said, "OH MY GOSH! YOU ARE SUPER HIGH!" I thought to myself, "Well, the gig is up." Then I rose to my feet, extended my hand and said, "Stephanie, my name is Aquarius. It has been a pleasure to meet you." I took two steps behind her, turned around and said, "Steph, by the way, I have no idea what you are talking about." I gave her a wink and a big smile then went outside.

When I walked outside toward my car and women everywhere were smoking cigarettes, buying food out of a vehicle vending machine and mostly chatting amongst themselves.

I come within five feet away from my car and there's four beautiful ladies standing around the parked vehicles besides mine. One of them said, "Hey, that is a nice car." I reply, "Thank you." Next, I proceed to have a seat and fired up the rest of the roach with my windows down and music blaring. Suddenly all four women totally surrounded my car and said, "Can we hit some of that!!???" So, I gave it to them and went back inside.

To my surprise Stephanie beat me back to our area. She was actually blocking me from passing her with her swivel chair. Upon approaching her, she stopped me and said, "You are fine!" I reply, "Thank you."

I liked her aggressiveness, but I have never been out with an older woman before. So, I was sort of leery. Yet on the other hand, in my mind, she was ready to look inside "The book!" So, I was seriously contemplating on sweeping this lady off her feet.

I sat down at the booth and made up my mind that I am not made to work. I pushed my swivel chair back, leaned over, and tapped Stephanie on the shoulder. Stephanie took off her headset in mid-sentence!

I asked her several questions so I could see where I could or would want to fit in. She was 38 years old, single, no kids, had her own place, a new car, and spent most of her time at work and home. She was well spoken, nice, and very polite. She stood about 5 feet 4 inches, weighed 130 pounds, and had good style. The main physical feature that stood out was her gigantic breast! For a moment, I started wondering why an older woman would want anything to do with a younger man. Then it dawned on me. SEX! So, since that is what she wanted, I figured I would toss her a little gesture signaling that I was equally attracted.

I asked her, "What size is your bra?" Her hazel eyes got big with excitement! with velocity she replied, "They are a 40 E." Obviously, they were her biggest assets, so why not show interest? Then I say, "Would you be interested in giving me your telephone number so that I could call you and arrange a time and a date to take a beautiful, young lady like yourself out?"

She pulled that pen out of her pocket like she just reached the 10th pace in a wild west shootout against dirty Clint Eastwood Harry himself! When the pen touched the paper, I could have sworn there was smoke illuminating from the surface. She did everything but blow the top of her pen and stuck it back into the holster.

We exchanged lustful looks and flirtatious body language for a few minutes. Then I told her that I would be calling her soon and would not return to this place. Then I left before quitting time.

Exactly two days later, I called Stephanie. She picked up the phone and said, "Hello?" I replied, "Hi, sexy, this is Aquarius. I was just calling to see if you were free Saturday night at 7pm?" Stephanie said, "Yes, do you have a pen and something to write on so I can give you my address and directions to my place?"

After a few minutes of pleasant conversation, we hung up the phone,

Saturday arrived extremely quick! During the previous days, I was strategically planning by making calls, shopping, and checking local listings.

Finally, I arrived at Stephanie's establishment. On the passenger's seat sat a dozen roses. There were 3 white, 3 yellow, 3 pink, and 3 red perfectly cut roses encased with white paper, and red ribbon. Inside the roses was a little card that I wrote on, saying: "Beautiful things belong to a gorgeous woman."

Also, along with the roses, was a tiny red, and white teddy bear, and a bottle of red wine.

I grabbed her gifts, closed the car door, and walked toward her front door. After ringing the doorbell, she answered three seconds later. To her surprise, she was wooed beyond her expectations. Stephanie said, "OH MY GOD! are these for me?" I said, "By golly yes they are most definitely are gorgeous."

I could already foresee the future and could tell that this woman would marry me, be a terrific wife, and have 15 kids if I wanted to. Mainly, due to her joyful reception, and appreciation of my gifts.

Stephanie, then invited me in while she put the flowers in a vase, placed the teddy bear besides them, and put the wine in her refrigerator. During all of this, my eyes were casing her place to get a better understanding of her.

After noticing that she was ready to see what else I had in store for her, I asked her if she was ready. She gleefully said yes.

During the drive, I asked her if she liked going to the theatres to watch movies. She said, "Oh my! I haven't gone out in 4 to 5 years, and it has been longer than that since I have been to a show." I immediately started to think to myself, "Where the hell has this woman been?" Then I said, "Well, you will like tonight then."

As we pulled up to the theaters, she said, "OH MY GOD! A drive-in movie???" I have never been to one of these in my entire life!" A quick thought arrived within me, Aquarius, you know what to do even when you are unsure boy! My seats in my car were more comfortable than most furniture at people's homes. Let alone some funky inside theatre.

As soon as we pulled up to pay, the cashier clerk looked inside the vehicle and said, "$10.00 please and turn your radio to dial 92.3. Enjoy all 3 films."

I had it in my mind that we would only watch two because there was one more place, I would like to take her.

When we pulled in, the place was semi packed. I spotted a secluded space far at the back. We parked the car and started to relax a bit. All the controls were on my side. So, I hit the power button that controlled her seat. It scared her as she said, "Oh!" I laughed as she slid further back. And then I reclined her a little so she could be perfectly comfortable.

The movie was about 5 minutes away from the beginning. I asked, "what would you like to drink?" Steph said, "It doesn't matter." I told her that I would be back with some refreshments in a moment. I walked for what seemed to be a quarter of a mile to the concession stand.

I order some chili dogs, pretzels, nachos, corn dogs, mozzarella sticks, 2 cheeseburgers, 2 bottled waters, M&M's, skittles, and 2 root beers. When I got back to the car with all of the food, she said, "Oh my goodness! who is going to eat all of that?" I said, "whatever you don't, I will! Besides, I wasn't aware of what you would like so I ordered it all." Stephanie smiled.

We left at 11:45 pm. and she thought the night was coming to an end. Sensing that, I said," "I know of a small little place about 20 minutes from here that I think you would like. Would you like to go?" Steph said, "Yes, I would love to go." That brought her spirits up. For a moment, I was feeling the exact same way she was sad and awkward.

We arrive at this small elegant bar, and dance place. She looked at me like, this is a little out of my league. I didn't think so though. there was a total of four people there. The bartender, bouncer, and mixed couple slow dancing on the dance floor to "In the Air" by Phil Collins.

We went straight to the bar and I told Stephanie to order anything and as much as she wanted to drink. The bartender took our orders. I ordered a corona and she ordered a whiskey sour. I have never ever heard of this drink. Now, I see that Stephanie is feeling a bit more comfortable knowing that no one is watching her and that this place is really laid back, she begins dancing and moving her neck back and forth. It could have been the drink.

After the 3rd drink, I expected her to stop, but no! She kept going and going! Whiskey sour after fucking whiskey sour! To me, it was $5 after mother fucking $5! I was overwhelmingly irritated. Not only had she dug a $50 hole in my pockets but now I know why she wasn't married and hasn't been out in a 1/2 a decade. She was an undercover classy drunk! Now, I am thinking that I have wasted my time on a classy drunk!

I am ready to go and have no intentions of calling her ever again. A 70's song came on and now she wants to dance. Even though I am furious as hell, I still give her this last request before returning to her home.

There is something about Romantic guys. Even though they see the date as a disaster, he will still woo you. We consider it experience learned and also practice for your true dates down the line.

During the drive to her place, Stephanie repeatedly thanked me and said that this was the best date she has ever been on and that she can see herself being with me, etc... I am thinking, "Well, if you weren't a classy ass drunk I could too! In return, I simply said, "Well, I am glad to contribute."

I pull up to her driveway. I get out of the car and opened her door, placed her left arm entwined with my right arm, and walked her to the front door of her home. Suddenly, I lied, "Stephanie, thank you for giving me the opportunity to take you out. It has been such a pleasure. Have a good night and I will be in contact with you." Even though it didn't go smoothly for me, I was too nice to tell her that truth.

Shockingly, Stephanie got aggressive on me! She said, "NO YOU DON'T! You are not getting off that easy!" she latched onto my arm like a pit bull, opened her front door and drug me inside. She said, "Now, I have a surprise for you! Make yourself feel at home and I will be back in a second." I am wondering what I should do. I decided to have a seat and wait to see what her surprise was going to be. I could at least do that.

I happened to turn to my left, and she appeared out of the hallway wearing some black high heels and a pink and white extra short negligee. My eyes damn near popped out of my head and my heart started racing in fear! THEN SHE SAID, "I will be in my bedroom waiting for you," then she turned and left. I leaned back and thought,

What in the hell just happened here?

The morale of the story is this, regardless of if I accepted her invitation to rape me or not, after I walked out that door, I had absolutely no intentions of keeping in contact. She would have taken it as a one-night stand that she would love to turn into a one lifespan.

My friend, if you came across the wrong "Mr. Romantic" your life could be turned upside down. This person's game is strong and filled with manipulating, deceptive illusions,

So be wise. Don't be gullible or naive to the cunning niceness of this person. Take your time, ask questions, and most importantly... "RECOGNIZE GAME!"

Chapter Four

The Platonic Friend Technique

Do you have a best friend? Have you ever thought of the reasons why that particular friend is the best out of all the ones you have? Without even knowing you personally, I can pinpoint several reasons why. 1.) They are easy to talk to 2.) You confide in them 3.) They are always there for you 4.) You trust their advice 5.) No matter what, they will never judge you.

The list could go on and on, but I will be willing to bet all the proceeds of this book that four out of five, named above pertains to you. If they do not describe your best friend, then you obtain a misconception on what qualifies or describes a best friend.

Before this peculiar individual approaches you, he will automatically think that you have been drugged through the ringer more than a few times. If that is not the case, he will imagine that you are a faithful woman already involved in a serious relationship. Furthermore, he will picture you as someone who knows that the only thing men are interested in is sex.

Any which way it goes, he has fabricated a technique to just get you to answer the door. If he can just get you to say, "Who is it?" He is confident enough to get you to put the chain on your door and open it to get a visual. Then after your body gets authorization from your thoughts, you will open the door, let him in, close the door, and locked it behind him.

How does he go about doing this? It is very simple, straightforward, and direct. Say for instance, you are at a mall or grocery store waiting in line either behind or in front of him. The line is long, you are in a hurry, pressed for time, or just bored. He will strike up a conversation quicker than a cobra will strike at a harmless rat! He will verbally voice and agree with your discomfort that the both of you are experiencing. That will pull you out of your shell and you will agree also. Then he will continue to discuss and ask you questions concerning irritations. I mean, hell, neither one of you don't know each other or care for the other but do have something in common at the moment...impatience.

You didn't even see him coming. Why? Because he didn't directly come on to you. This approach comes indirect.

After the preliminary, he will say, "By the way, my name is so and so and I just got out of a serious relationship. I have no interest in pursuing another one anytime soon, but I would like to be your friend, if you have any openings available."

The ball is in your court now and you will accept, due to the fact, he was honest and upfront. Well, that is what you think. You will start to justify and reason with yourself, There is nothing wrong with having a friend. I am not attracted to him, and neither is he toward me. He seems cool and honest. Why not?

Part two of the game has now began. This person is so into you that he is willing to become your friend, first! He will get you talking about yourself, and your entire life because he really wants to know. You see, information entrusted in the wrong person could get you!

Question? Can a person automatically know you unless you tell them? Right! If you are speaking to him about the current problems in your relationship with your boyfriend, he will know when it will end, what to do, and what not to do when it becomes his time to fill in the blanks.

You, being unconsciously aware, have become an instructor. If someone is seeking to learn a new trade, first they will have to be

THE PLATONIC FRIEND TECHNIQUE

willing to learn. (Honestly, I haven't met a woman who doesn't want to be understood. That means women love to teach! Every dance instructor, teacher, professor, or mother has a favorite specimen, and can foresee their favorite specimen's future and how far they are going to go in life.

There is a saying that goes like this, you don't have to be looking, it will come looking for you. It doesn't matter if it is trouble, money, or love. It is not what happens to you that counts, but your reactions to it.

In the same manner, Mr. Platonic really isn't Mr. Platonic at all. He is a wolf in sheep's clothing, hiding behind a mask. He has only two ways to attack you. 1.) By waiting for the perfect tie to reveal his motives of being your friend from in the first place. Basically, seizing the opportunity. 2.) By waiting for you to exhaust all your options and by doubting your choice selection of men. Then contemplate on being the first, proactive person to step beyond the boundaries of your verbal agreement by suggesting an attempt towards a serious relationship addition to the clause.

The second strategy works best for him because he will get to keep his ulterior motives hidden behind the "platonic masks" while you play yourself! All that he has to do is keep the platonic role going, do whatever you hint at, and not do whatever it was the previous 2, 3, 4, or 5 guys did to end the relationship. This technique could go on for however long he decides.

Allow me to give you two excerpts from my previous personal experience using this technique...

It was a sunny day outside. Approximately,90 degrees with a slight 5 mile per hour breeze. The sun was shining bright and there were hardly any clouds up in the bright, blue sky. It was one of those perfect days to have a nice walk.

There was a popular local seven eleven located around the corner from this apartment complex I was visiting. So, I decided to take a little stroll up to the convenient store. For one, I was extremely thirsty. Secondly, I was excessively eager to meet a few of the multitudes of women frequently coming and exiting the store.

I was wearing a red, New York Yankee 7 1/4, fitted baseball cap, a white buttoned up polo, unbuttoned with my a-shirt underneath, some beige polo khakis shorts, and some white polo canvas shoes with no socks, I would consider that the casual summer attire.

As I turn the corner, a carload of women rode by waving and honking at me. (at that point in time they were lucky they didn't stop because I was definitely up to no good.) So, I kept walking towards my destination. Finally, after about 3 minutes or so I opened the door to see a store full of women. There were different kinds of candy everywhere! I thought to myself as I entered, "I chose the perfect time to take a walk!"

Bam! After a quick observation of the entire store my homing device beamed in on a target. She was about 25 years of age, outrageously tanned, stood 5 ft. 5 inches, and weighed 120 pounds. She had long, silky, straight, black hair that dangled in the middle of her back. Her green eyes reminded me of the artificial green grass in kids Easter basket. Her toes and fingernails were French manicured and all! She also was wearing an A-shirt, some tight, red, gym shorts, and some white thong sandals. It looked like she was fixing to go to the lake or something. This lady was drop dead gorgeous!

The only thing was that her attitude spoke volumes, DO NOT EVEN THINK ABOUT SPEAKING TO ME. I AM NOT IN THE MOOD FOR ANYONE'S BULLCRAP!

Ha! To me she was way to fine for me to listen to her body language, and my need to get her attention far outweighed anything she was feeling momentarily. I batted a thousand no matter what type of a pitch that any pitcher threw. I am going to hit a home run, I thought to myself.

I B-lined to the drink section to retrieve a watermelon and grape Snapple. Then, rudely cut everyone in line and tossed the cashier two one-dollar bills for the drink that cost $1.49 and told her to keep the change. I pissed off everyone in line including the gorgeous target. I was not going to wait in line for one item, and I had to beat the object of my affection out the door so I can execute my sales pitch in a professional manner, one on one.

As soon as I exited the seven eleven double doors, I made a left and took 10 steps toward the pay phone. I fumbled threw my pockets for some change to make a quick page (long time ago, I know!) and the next thing you know, caught totally off guard, the beautiful lady trotted up beside me to use the connecting telephone.

Coincidence or not, my level of confidence is at an all-time high! So, after I place a call, I pace my left, bottom foot against the wall, lean back all cool like I am posing for a photo, and toss back my delicious Snapple while waiting patiently to catch this fish.

She spoke into the phone for two to three minutes, hung up, and did everything but ran towards her car. As soon as I picked up on her velocity, I acted as a roadblock and said, "Excuse me" she stopped and gave me a look that said, "Mother fucker!, If you don't get out of my way, I am going to knock you out!" Seeing this hideous look, I chuckled and said, "Damn, you are a feisty thing, but anyways, I was hoping that we could become friends, no sex included."

The no sex included statement was the best thing I could have said because when those hit her ear drums then registered in her brain her look changed to, What? You aren't interested in having sex with me? Her shoulders dropped and all the tension seemed to have left her entire body. Then she said, "My name is Angela. Do you have a pen and something to write on so I can give you my number?"

Ha! Angela was so ready to give me the sex that she didn't even care to ask me my name! She was the type that absolutely hated men coming on to her. She liked to pick, choose, and be the aggressor. All I did was present to her the opportunity and like a fat juicy worm being dangled in front of a hungry catfish, she took the bait.

So, I neglected to give her my name and pulled out a rolodex I could program her information. Angela said, "Oh! You come prepared don't cha?" I replied, "You cannot trust loose paper and you will never know when you will run into someone important."

Now she becomes inquisitive by asking, "Well, are you going to call me here after a while? If you aren't busy, maybe I could come over?"

Do you see how the turn of events changed drastically? It is almost as if she heard me say, "If you come over tonight, we would have sex."

What if I was serious about not having sex? Regardless, if I was or wasn't, I was determined to tantalize her anyways. S I said, "I will call you at 7:45p.m. and give you the directions to my house." We said our goodbyes and dispersed.

What she didn't know was that she was going to be coming over another female friends' home, and she was going to be present. If I were to actually be alone with her at my house, the possibility of us having lascivious sex would have been great! Furthermore, would it really matter who's house it was, and who would be there since I verbally stated the "no sex clause?"

*This next example is a tad bit different.... This is an episode of "Mr. Platonic vs. Ms. May"

Me and my friend April have been good friends for a little over two years. Our relationship was strictly platonic. Neither one of us ever thought about making a pass at each other or anything of that nature. We could go to one another's home at any time of the night, regardless of our monogamous partner is there or not. If either one of us needed a place to stay, money, or any favor, we would be there for another. No if's, and's, or but's about it.

April was a few years older than I. We both did it with one of our friends, and she knew that I was a player. Up until this moment, she has never had a boyfriend, but this particular individual caused her to fall in love.

I used to be able to walk straight into her house unannounced, until her boyfriend moved in. It all happened so sudden, you know? Sometimes April and I wouldn't see each other or even speak for two or three months. Not that anything was the matter with our friendship, it was just we had busy lives. We had that type of understanding and nothing has changed because of it.

Then, out of the blue, well, even out of the orange, not only does April have a boyfriend, but he has moved in and is controlling her place??!! It did more than threw me for a loop! It totally shocked the hell out of me! Plus, I wasn't notified. We were closer than this! That is what made it all seem so odd to me.

One day I walked straight through April's front door, like usual, after a 3-month hiatus, and a mysteries person leaped up from the sofa into a taekwondo defense posture. He was Mexican, stood 5 ft 9 inches tall, and weighed about 200 pounds. He had shoulder length hair, and a thick goatee. He was wearing some black 1992 Corridor Kroger sack house shoes, black Dickie's hanging halfway off his butt, and a blue and black flannel jacket on. He looked like a California Mexican gang banger.

We are in Oklahoma City, Oklahoma and this type of dress is sort of outdated and inappropriate in this day in age. April was a long, blonde hair, blue eyed, big breasted white girl. I figured her taste in men was more the middle to upper class, bourgeois, suburban type, like my friend she is sleeping with. Better yet, more of someone like myself.

So, I am standing in the entrance baffled. Swiftly, April comes darting in-between us like a referee at the start of a boxing match separating us by spreading her arms, palms up. Next, she said, "Tiger, this is my good friend, Aquarius. Aquarius, this is my boyfriend, Tiger." Then, Tiger turns to April and says, "Is this how you let people come into your house? Well, you better tell him that from her on out, as long as I am here, this isn't going to happen no more." I add in my two cents, "Tiger, calm down. I don't mean any harm, nor disrespect. I didn't know that you lived here. From now on, I will knock or ring the doorbell, okay?" Tiger replied, "It's cool." Finally, April apologized to the both of us, due to the fact, she should have forewarned us both concerning the new situation.

After that mild altercation, I still continuously dropped by April and Tigers place. April, Tiger, and I became quite cool. Besides his appearance, on the inside he was not that bad of a guy. He treated April good, and she seemed to be happier, so all is well and ends well.

Recently, I went on another 3-month hiatus. I just happened to be in April's neighborhood, so I decided to swing by and hang out with the new couple. I rang the doorbell and heard April's voice scream, "Come in!" Upon entering, I see April sitting on the couch looking sad and depressed. I ask her, "Sweetheart, what is the matter?" April replied, "Tiger got his probation revoked and two weeks ago he went back to prison for 1 year." I thought to myself, Damn!

So, I consoled her and attempted to make her feel better. She was a good girlfriend. She hung out with his family, visited, and sent him money every week. This carried on for 3 months.

Then the final night came. You know, in the past, our common denominator was marijuana. April was a hustler, too! I'd always pop up to blow or match her with some different kinds of weed.

I was out, but something told me that she wasn't. So, one night after the club, I stopped by April's house to see if she would smoke one with me. It didn't matter that it was 3 am. Seventy five percent of the time, that is the time I went over there anyways.

When I pulled up in her driveway, I noticed all her lights were out. So, I knocked on the door, lightly because I really didn't want to wake her up if she was sleeping. No matter how bad I wanted to get high.

She opened the door and I said, "why is it all dark around here, girl?" She smiled and said, "Aquarius, Come on in! I didn't want people to think I was here" You see, April had a lot of people coming over to her place.

Next, she said, "Have a seat." Then I said, "April, are you high? Because you sure are acting different!" April replied, "Aquarius, I just got a hold of some tropical" I bent down to take a closer look at April's eyes, and they were bloodshot red for real! April smiled at me and then leans back deeper into her couch. I then said, "Tropical? What in the hell is Tropical??" She said, "Aquarius this weed is so good that the only word to describe it is Tropical."

Note that we are sitting in darkness! The only light being the light coming through the living room window for the moon. This whole scenario is weird. The entire 4 to 5 years I have been visiting my friend, I have never experienced this. I started getting nervous butterflies, scared, and anxious simultaneously! I am unsure if I should take one toke of this "Tropical" stuff April has.

Next thing you know, April bent over, reached between her legs, and pulled a tray out from underneath the couch. She slid the tray over to me. It had two or three different zig zags, two lighters, ash tray, and a sandwich bag a quarter full of marijuana.

Turning to my right, I said, "April, sweetie can we get just a little light in here?" She retorted, "Oh! I am so sorry. Let me light this candle." Now, I am hoping that this stuff doesn't fry my brain because April is totally out of her element.

After the itsy-bitsy candle was lit, and placed on the tray, this is when I saw the substance. Believe me when I tell you this weed looked like it was straight out of a high times magazine. It looked like a fluorescent green mini asteroid with bright white speckles on them.

So, I twist one up, leaned back, placed the joint in my mouth, and fired it up. Do you remember the 1970's batman show? Well, back then, every time Batman or Robin hit someone or got hit words would appear on the television screen used as an illustration, describing the impact of the fist.

Well, that is what happened to me. As soon as that smoke hit my lungs, "BAM! WHAM! BOOM! ZAP! My brain felt like it was being hit by Mike Tyson when he was in his prime! My eyeballs got extremely heavy, tongue dried up quicker than a drop of water touching a hot skillet, and my thoughts started to go beyond its normal pattern. Then, suddenly, I couldn't feel my entire body!

All I did was sit there and watch the clock do from 3:20 to 3:30 to 3:45 to 4:00 am while the joint faded out in my right hand in between my thumb and index finger.

Finally, after 40 minutes of being paralyzed, I turned to April and said, "Girl, this is some tropical!" April replied, "Aquarius, pass the tropics and lets smoke!" So, I complied.

Ten minutes went by and when I sat the joint in the astray, I said, "April, have ever thought about me and you ever getting together?" It felt like it took me 3 minutes to say those words. Especially, how slow I was speaking. April kind of snapped out of her comatose state of mind for a split second. Her eyelids batted ferociously, and her eyes got really big like I shocked her with a quiz.

Immediately, with a puzzled look on her face, she said, "What do you mean?" High as the sky, I said, "You know, me and you?" April said, "I really haven't thought about it. That is a good question." Obviously, that tropical weed had me feeling tropical for real because in hindsight, if I wasn't high from that stuff, I wouldn't have asked her that question. I wasn't the only one feeling a tad bit tropical when April said, "Aquarius, I already know that you are terrific in bed. My friend Sissy told me all about it."

The next thing you know, she was on her feet taking her clothes off and telling me to follow her to the bedroom.

So, my dear friend, unless you want to get played, ignore all the warnings, facts, and personal illustrations written about in this chapter. Don't say that I didn't tell you so. It'll be better for you now than later to... RECOGNIZE GAME!

Chapter Five

THE UNDERCOVER PIMP PLOT

Since most of the world is so adamant on accepting the tidal waves of recession, a lot of civilians are going to be faced with gargantuan obstacles to overcome, such as financial situations, relationships, and morals just to name a few.

To this obscure individual, he no longer must fish in creeks or ponds. He has graduated from his usual project, section 8 type of female, and moved toward the young, separated, single, middle class failing mother, who is experiencing a life crisis.

Have you ever thought about what is going through the mind of a car salesman? First, without a customer, there will be no sale, so when a person comes strolling in the car lot, he knows that you are interested in purchasing a vehicle. Secondly, without a sale, he does not receive any type of commission. So, regardless if you are just browsing or not, he is going to persuade, motivate, inspire, manipulate, con, lie, and try his best to get you to buy a car. Basically, he is thinking, I must get them by any means necessary! Failure is not an option.

Well, the only difference between the car salesman and the undercover pimp is, the car buyer has somewhat of a clue on what they are getting into, and who they are dealing with, and the latter doesn't.

When you think of the word pimp, these things may come to mind: stylish, flamboyant, flashy, full of pizzazz. He has the colorful suits, big diamond rings, and the foreign or the American expensive cars just speaking on his outer appearance that is what you would think of. When describing his character, I am sure that we could come up with all kinds of derogatory statements, but what if the person lost all his outer flamboyancy? At least, with the flashy pimp you could see him a mile away. This is the main reason for this chapter. It is to help the financially strapped and financially desperate women to identify... "The Undercover Pimp."

This is how the undercover pimp came about his knowledge to go undercover.

Opposites do not attract! That is the biggest, farthest from the truth lie that is stampeding the earth. When the former flamboyant and colorful pimp was roaring like a lion, looking for some prey, trying to catch a potential or experienced prostitute was extremely difficult. For one, the experienced prostitutes were scared and avoided him because they already had a pimp or was scared to leave their pimp and go be with him because it would be a major risk. Due to comfort, even if she wanted to be with him, who is to say that the living situations would be better? Better yet, who is to say that if they were better things wouldn't change for the worse?

On the other hand, the non-experienced prostitute (or one who is unaware of her potential to become one) does not have the foreknowledge like the experienced one, but when encountering this colorful pimp, an alarm does go off in her gut.

Deep down inside, she knows he is somewhat different but not really. She is attracted to what she thinks, and he just happens to manifest her thoughts in the physical.

Internally, they are also the same, but she is a tad bit scared. He is a risk taker and adventurous. She is unsure about what adventures he will take her on.

He will sense this, "I want to, but I don't know" aura extruding from her all because of his flamboyance. Dressing like a pimp attracts a lot of women but getting them to take a dangerous road is a whole different story.

Basically, he has come to acknowledge that If he downgrades his outer appearance, he will automatically strip the warning, yield, and stop signs off of his chest. Then he can get down to business. The only set back (which it doesn't really matter) is that he is going to have to take the offensive approach instead of being stalked or chose.

That alone has its obstacles because a lot of people (male and female) are shallow. If he downsizes too much, no matter what comes flying out of his mouth the other person is not going to hear one word. Regardless, of the fact the end justifies the means. The wise probability percentage is 50% higher this way.

The Undercover Pimp chooses victims sporadically due to their financial need. Say for instance, he pulls into a gas station and spots an attractive, young lady getting out of an old beat up car with three children, automatically, he will know she is struggling. Especially, if she is single. The kids must eat, have clothes, may need to see a doctor, go to a day car, and some more. Plus, there are several bills to pay and her car is unreliable.

The pimp knows she needs help and have sat up many nights worrying and stressing over tomorrow's finances. Furthermore, since she is attractive and has 3 kids, to him she likes sex and more than likely has been contemplating on selling herself just for her children's sake.

The pimp knows she needs help, by the sacrifices that she has made, to figure out a quick and fast solution to her problems. Basically, she has catapulted herself into a drastically desperate situation.

All along, during the temporary separation, the pimp is feeling the same exact way the victim does. Mainly, because they are both desperate for money and how money will solve their problems.

The victim has the body and the pimp has the brain along with the manly protection. Without each other, their main objective will not be reached.

Mr. Undercover Pimp will not waste his time. Yet, he needs to see how bad off her living conditions are. After receiving confirmation, he will shoot his sales pitch of himself, first. He has to make sure that she is sold on him wanting to have a long-term relationship with her before he lets the other face appear.

This individual knows that she is sick of short-term relations because it is the reason why she is in this predicament in the first place, he also knows that, with 3 children, no man is going to want her. He will touch on that topic but will make himself appear to be willing to accept, clean up, and better the situations circumstances.

Finally, the suggestions arise to the surface. I know a few women who used to escort. They were in a position that you are in now, but after a couple of weeks, they made 10k. If I were you, I would consider doing the same thing. I would understand and wouldn't look at you any different. Bam! Mr. Subtle wittingly and cunningly just finessed her into acting on her own thoughts.

Not only does she get to maintain a relationship but gets to make some quick cash along with some immoral support. Yes, it is nefarious, but it works.

*Please allow me to give you a paradigm into a similar situation, concerning my past experience....

This situation occurred on the south west side of Oklahoma City. One third of the population are seriously struggling. Another third is barely making ends meet. While the other 33.3% is coasting along and doing quite well financially. So, 66.6% of the entire South West side of Okc need help!

It is summertime in July and the weather is perfect. There is hardly any wind blowing or any clouds in the sky. It seems like the entire state is out and about, driving to and fro.

Here I am, a lion, sitting behind the wheel of a cherry red convertible Ford Mustang looking for some prey. My intentions are entirely different from the normal, "Hey, what's up? Wanna go out, party, get drunk and have some lascivious sex?" type mentality. I am crawling (cruising) the streets (jungle) searching for the perfect specimen (deer/potential prostitute.)

After combing the southwest sides main streets going east to west (15th, 29th, 44th, 59th) to no avail, I decided to comb the streets going south to north (May, Penn, western, and walker.)

After a strenuous hour and a half and a half tank of petroleum, I arrived at the next to last stoplight before I turn onto the highway and headed to the north west side to try my luck.

So, while I am sitting there at the stop light waiting for the light to change, I begin thinking, "Damn! all the girls cruising around here are all lustful minded instead of money minded. What a waste of a day, and what a waste of their body!"

As the light turned green, I took one deep breath to shake off the frustration and took off toward the highway.

Keep in mind, even though it seemed like I have conceded, I am desperately hoping to spot a chic during these last 15 blocks. The speed limit was 35 miles per hour. I was going 20 mph. I am in total shock because this side of town had the easiest fish in it.

Blinking my eyes furiously, my falcon vision keener in on a female winking approximately 217.7 feet ahead of me. My testosterone and adrenaline shot through my entire body! My right foot suddenly got extremely heavy as I saw her make a left into an apartment complex.

I swooped down on her like a vulture on a dead carcass! I turned left into the apartment complex and sped down to where she was now heading up the stairs. I finally reached her exactly as she as fumbling in her purse and said, "Excuse me, could you tell me how to get to the north west side of town?"

She came back down the stairs and stood directly in front of my driver's side door. She had long, black, straight hair that hung about an inch below her butt. Her green eyes reminded me of the color of money. Her skin was beige colored, and she stood about 5 ft. 8 inches. I am guessing her age was about 22 or 23 years old. She was also wearing a subway uniform. I took it that she just got off from work.

My thoughts were calculating up all the facts. Young, attractive, had a poverty-stricken job, and no car. I need more information in order to detect which angle I should attack.

With a voice full of depression, the woman said, "Well, you go back up to the entrance, make a left, and go underneath the bridge, make another left on the highway, and take the north Okc exit." I said,

"Thanks, Laura." (Her name tag was pinned to her shirt.)

A tad bit perplexed, Laura said, "How do you know my name?" I replied, "It is written in bold black print on your name tag." Laura blushed, then she said, "I am so sorry if I came off like a bitch. It has been a long week, and I have a lot on my mind."

Bingo! She opened the door wide open for me to come in and help save her problems. Actually, that was her first mistake. (You should never open yourself up like that to a total stranger.)

So, since I sensed desperation, I skipped all the small talk, and said, "Laura, I am not really that big of a hurry to go to the north west side. My name is Aquarius. If you aren't busy, and need a friend to talk to, I would be more than happy to come up and listen to your problems. Maybe I could help you out."

Laura bit for it like a big mouth bass! She replied, "No. I am not busy, and I don't have anywhere to go or anything to do. Come on up." I parked the car, let the top down, and got out of the car.

After the three flights of stairs, we finally arrived at her apartment door. Laura inserted the key and twist the doorknob and opened the door. What engulfed my eyeballs was astonishing there was one brown loveseat and one dusty ole end table through her entire living room and kitchen area.

From the looks of things, it seemed that Laura was doing worse than I thought! I quickly erased the ecstatic look off my face and walked in her place like there was nothing missing. I took a seat and propped my feet on her itsy-bitsy table, while she closed the door and opened her blinds to let in some light. Automatically, I start thinking, do not tell me that she doesn't have any electricity! Damn! I think I have hit the jackpot!

Next, she turned to me and said, "I don't have the money to turn the electric on." I said, "It doesn't bother me, I have been there before." I was starting to feel awful for Laura. A part of me wanted to leave and the devious part of me wanted to turn her out! So, I ended up staying and submitting to the manipulating voice.

Laura didn't waste any time whatsoever! Immediately, she sat down next to me and said, "I sure do appreciate you taking the time to hang out with me. I just moved here a month ago from Kansas. I don't have any friends, no car, no money, and I just got a 72-hour eviction notice. Plus, I have only been working this job for a week and it pays every two weeks. I don't have a clue of what I am going to do."

Damn! This must be fate! I started to think, she doesn't have any other choice but to sell her soul to the devil. Then, I hear the good angel on my right shoulder say, "Aquarius, it is good to help, but will you really be helping her or making her situation worse, all for the sake of the money?"

So, I am in a state of shock and I am overwhelmed with a sense of guilt. For one, empathizing with Laura was heart breaking. Secondly, I was feeling like I was taking advantage of her by what I was seriously contemplating to do.

Suddenly, overwhelmed with indecision, I rose up and said, "I am going to call a few friends of mine. Then, if you are not busy, I will come back over here later tonight, OK?" The look on Laura's face makes me feel like I was going to abandon her. At this junction, for her sake, I was leaning toward the good voice.

Finally, Laura said, "You are not really going to come back, are you?" I replied, "I promise you that I will be here no later than 8 pm, okay?" Laura said, "Well, I hope so. I am sick of being here all by myself and all lonely and shit!" After that, I walked out of the door.

After a few leisure hours of doing absolutely nothing, I decided to head back over to Laura's residence. I figured some time away from the situation would catapult me into coming to a conclusion. Instead, the only conclusion I came up with was that I wasted several hours of precious time because I was in the exact same undecided predicament.

Prior to pulling to Laura's apartment building, I saw that her porch light was off. Plus, there wasn't any sign of life emanating from her living quarters at all! Then it dawned on me, Damn! I forgot that she didn't have any electricity! She couldn't be in there just sitting in the dark.

In my heart and mind, I am hoping she has left or something. I am searching for any reason for me to avoid walking those steps toward her door. To me, it didn't seem logical for anyone to be living like this. Regardless, of the opinion, I had to keep my word and at least check and see if Laura was sitting in the dark.

I rang the doorbell. Oops! There is no power! I let loose from the rapid taps on her door. About 10 seconds elapsed without a response. Normally, I would be very adamant, but this was not the case. Immediately, I turned around and walked away speedily. About halfway down the stairs, I had a door open and a voice say, "Aquarius!"

I come to a halt. I turned around slowly and saw Laura standing halfway out of her door, draped in a white bath towel, waving for me to come back up.

Let's pause for a second. Okay, you are a woman. Can you believe this shit? This is a 1,000% true story and by me just recalling this memory makes me ponder its validity!

I went back up the stairs and entered the quiet, cold, and extremely dark dungeon of an apartment. Laura said, " Stand right there while I light this candle so we can see. I reached in my pocket to retrieve a lighter and guess what else I came up with? Yep, a forgotten quarter sack of some fire ass refers!

I apologize to you, but I was going through some very stressful times and wasn't aware with how to deal with the stress. So, I turned to the "grass" so to speak. During this incident, I turned to her quicker than an overly scorned woman who turns on her newly found creating husband!

After the tiny candle was lit, we sat down on the love seat. I rolled up a joint and took several hard and aggressive tokes. Laura looked at me like I was deranged.

A few idle babblings protruded from her voice box that sounded like opera music to me, because this refer had me pretty high. A couple of " Mmm, hmmm's, and oh yea's came out of my mouth. Then it seemed like another person emerged from within me.

Now, I am looking her up and down, examining the provocative towel she is wearing. For a female who is hours away from being homeless, she doesn't seem to be worried too much about it now, for some odd reason.

It could have been the stimulant, but it seemed like her boobs got bigger and her legs got longer. Either that or the towel was super short!

Next, I finally zoomed in on what she was talking about. Laura said, "I just want to be held, caressed and loved." What in the hell???" I thought. Were in the world was this leading to? I cannot lie, her body was calling my name in English, Spanish, German, French, and Arabic! I didn't even know I spoke fluently in four other languages!

Furthermore, Laura suggested that we should make a mat on the floor so I could hold and caress her. The situation seemed to get tighter and tighter as the seconds ticked by. I felt an anger sensation beginning to arise. All this physical touching and nonsense was not part of the deal. So, out of pure anger, I popped the question, "You can make at least 2k by becoming a call girl for one day. I have a lot of female friends who are doing it as we speak. Are you interested?"

To my cotton-picking surprise, Laura was not thrown off at all by the question. It was almost as if she wanted to be a prostitute but didn't want to go at it alone. She simply answered, "As longs as you are with me, I will."

Damn! Damn! Damn! What a life!" As I thought to myself. So, now being filled with glee, I tell her to go and get that blanket and let's make a pallet on the floor.

You see, my dear lady friend, it is vitally important for you to consider absorbing this valuable information. For you, to study the character, identity, morals, and mistakes of Laura. Secondly, to pinpoint the subtlety, wittiness, and craftiness of the proactive hunter. Last but not the least, in totality to... RECOGNIZE GAME!

Chapter Six

THE SEX FIEND STRATEGY

Are you one of those distinct individuals who think that sex is a major part of a relationship? Well, let me ask you these questions. How many sexual partners have you had in your lifetime? Did you keep them all? How long did your so-called relationships last? Are you currently single?

There is an old saying that goes something like this, if your actions do not produce your desired result, consider changing your way of thinking. You see, if that way of thinking were correct, you wouldn't be lonely, single, feeling used, or even had multiple sex partners. Please, do not get me wrong, sex is a part of relationship it is just not "THE" major part of it.

Men and women think totally different. I won't generalize it, so I will say that most of the gorgeous, fine, pretty, and sexy women "know" they can get any man they want, due solely upon their outer appearances. From a man's point of view, I could agree with that, but the key word in that previous sentence was- "GET." Notice that I didn't use the word- "KEEP."

Most of the handsome, good looking, and attractive men are sort of the same way. The major difference between the two, (which I think that you will agree) is they will lie. The question is, "Why do men lie?"

Well, it is so simple that it flies right over the top of women's heads! It is because they want to "LIE" down with you!

Women use sex for love. Men use your love for sex!

Most of the men that I know, look at a female as a whore when she sleeps with him so fast. Why? Because in his mind, he is thinking, "If she slept with me that fast, she has probably done it or will do it again and again with someone else!" He may continue lying to you in order to continue lying down with you because you may have been a tremendous lay, but he won't take you seriously.

Even though you are not the type that sleeps around it only takes that one time to label you one. My advice to this individual is to cross your legs, maintain sex control, and make him wait at least 6 months. That is if you really want a long-term commitment. In that time frame, you will be able to study his true behavioral patterns. If his intensity of interest decreases, throw him in the garbage. If it remains steady over that long period of time or intensifies, you might want to consider giving him a sample test of what I would like to call a trial run. If it is successful, then consider marrying him.

To my gorgeous, sexy, pretty, and fine women, do you want to know why it seems like all the good men are taken? It is because all the inwardly beautiful women are swooping them up from right underneath your nose!

These category of women makes the good man feel secure in his decision of selecting the right woman for both of their purposes in life. This type of woman's beauty is going to come forth shining bright like the sun! Therefore, becoming more attractive and more beautiful on the outside.

To the man, more than likely, this couple started off friends. (Mainly, due to her outer appearance, which wasn't a bad thing.) Then as time passed, and she really got to know the person, her inner beauty started to encamp around him like a fog. He started breathing in her radiances and before you know it, she won the #1 prize. Her self-respect, standards, morals, goals, and patients won him over.

If you dress provocatively and look tastier than a 12-ounce T-Bone steak, you can rest assured that you will attract wolves!

Say, for instance, that is exactly what you are wanting. Your mindset is, I am single, independent woman and the only thing a man is good for is sex. Also think I am going to wear this fiery tight-fitting red dress out to the club, shake my ass, and go home with a good-looking man.

One question, have you ever went shopping for a particular item and accidentally found something better and cheaper than the item you previously had your mind set on? Well, I ask that you say this, you may think that you are inferior, irresistible, hard, core, and are not buying what any man is selling, but are only looking for a quick scratch until you find out you accidentally stumbled across a diamond in the rough?

All your preceding sexual encounters were mild, cool, okay, and some a little above average. Some rides were disappointing, some you had to fake, and some took too long for you to reach your orgasmic sensation.

Then you unknowingly met your match! Not only did you get overwhelmingly turned on, but he turned you completely out! This person did things to you that you were unaware that would help you reach climax. He totally rocked your entire world! He made your volcano erupt multiple times! It happened quickly and it did not stop. It even kept going after the sexual encounter ceased.

This guy's whole aim in life is to be the 1st person to truly give you the ultimate sexual experience of your life! He is completing with himself. His goal is to blow your mind quicker and harder than the first, second, third, fourth, and fifth orgasm he has given you, but in all one setting!

There won't be any neglected body part. Every millimeter of skin and crevices would be kissed, touched, rubbed, licked, and sucked just the way you couldn't imagine.

You could be 60 years of age and still think that he just took your virginity! There is no coming back from that. It just like that saying once a white female goes black, she will never go back."

Since you quickly opened your legs to the new millennium penis methamphetamines, you will chase that high for a very long time. This person is fully aware of what he has done to you. Just like the person who did heroin for the first time, you will do whatever it takes to get that wonderful feeling again. This guy uses sex as a weapon!

Please allow me to adorn you with a personal illustration from my old, previous life....

I made a routine stop at a local Circle K to fill my tank up with some gasoline so I could continue patrolling the streets, in search of some hot women. I don't usually pay for things like gas, or fuel, die to having women pay for it, but since I was on the wrong side of town, I was forced to do it.

I was in a hurry, so I opened the gas tank, put the nozzle in and rushed into the store. As soon as I entered, I noticed that the cashier was not present. "Oh well." I thought and kept walking toward the fountain drink section to get a 64-ounce strawberry soda pop to quench my thirst. The store seemed awfully quiet and dead for 2 pm. After retrieving my drink, I turn around and spotted some Funyuns chips and grabbed those also and headed toward the counter.

The store was filled with all sorts of goodies. On the way to the counter, I saw the candy section. I most definitely had to get some peanut butter cups. That is when I saw her! The cashier lady had on a red uniform and a white tag on the left pocket jacket. Behind the counter, besides her big, blue eyes, the only thing visual was her long, candy blonde hair.

She was looking at me in a weird way. First, I could tell that she was kind of shy, naive, and gullible. The first thought I had was, "I wonder if she will let me get all of this stuff for free?"

I went to the counter and said, "What up, Tina? Do you think I could get my gas for free?" Tina said, "Dang! You are bold. I don't even know your name." I replied, "I apologize. How rude of me. My name is Aquarius. Do you think it is possible that I could get these items for free, also?" Tina started laughing and, "Oh my you just automatically know that I was going to let you get your gas free, huh?" I said, "Yep! Because you seem like a very nice person." She smiled and said, "Boy go ahead."

That was my cue. There was some beef jerky on the counter, so I said, "How about this box of 24, too?" Again, Tina said, "I don't care."

Hell, I knew that I was pushing it, but I wanted one more item. So, I pushed on, "One more thing, sweetheart, and I swear to you I will leave after this." Tina nodded.

I walked toward the alcohol section and grabbed a 24 pack of bud light and went back to the counter. Tina said, "Damn! You are going to get me into trouble!" I replied, "This is it. I promise. Give me your number, too I will call you later after you get off work." She gave me her number, I grabbed the items and left.

Six months have passed. During that time, Tina and I hung out a lot. Some of the time was spent at her house and the other time was at mine. We introduced each other to our crazy friends, watched movies, went to restaurants, and shopped a lot together.

During that entire time, neither one of us asked about each other's dating life or even made any physical contact at one another. Tina just thought I was crazy and just like hanging out with me.

Then, all of a sudden, totally out of nowhere, Tina came over to my house at noon. She walked in and took a seat clear on the other side of the living room as usual. I looked at her and said to myself, Damn! What is wrong with me? It has been 6 months and I haven't even made a move on this woman. She has been cool. I better reward her for being cool. Then I blurted out, "Tina! Would you like to have sex with me?" Very nonchalantly, Tina said, "Yeah."

I stood up stretched out my right hand for her to grab. Tina walked toward it and placed her hand gently into mine. Her hand was extremely soft.

As we walked down the hallway, we took a left into the bedroom. I was kind of nervous, but AI shook it off because it was time to perform. So, I put on my sex-ray vision and looked Tina's body over from head to toe.

She was well tanned. She had some pretty hands with natural nails, with white polish. She had on a long, white skirt and red sequin top on.

As she stood there in front of me, I now could not help but notice her breast were huge! So, I said, "what size bra do your wear?" Tina replied, "a 38 G." I have always been into pretty hands, cute toes, and big breasted women, but these breast here were the biggest I have gotten to see, touch, and kiss by far!

The weird thing was that she just stood there. Then it dawned on me that since we met, she just does whatever I tell her to. So, I took it like she was the type that loved to be told what to do! I had no problem with it because I loved giving orders!

So, I took off my shirt so she could see what was about to be rubbing all over her. then I tell her to take off all of her clothes and come get in bed with me. (Remember, its broad daylight and this is my first sexual encounter in the daytime.) Tina broke out of her clothes like they had fire all over them and glided across the floor towards the bed.

I won't go into detail, but after two hours of heart pounding, eye rolling, sweat pouring, and multiple orgasmic sensations, Tina laid on her back with her two legs propped up, holding her heart, and while having convulsions! For a second, I thought she was having a mild seizure and I was going to have to put my foot behind her head in order to keep her from swallowing her tongue.

Then she said, "OMG! The whole time I felt like the world was shaking!" I smiled and thought, "Another on bites the dust!"

Two years, several upon several thousands of dollars, a new car, and multiple upon multiple shopping sprees later, our relationship ended, due to the exposure of my other lady friends.

So, my dear friend, know that, "Patience is the weapon that forces deception to repeal itself." Consider filing this into your memory back, too. "God never intended for us to be having sex outside of marriage anyways! Just look around and be observant. Do you see all the single mothers? How about all the aids, H.I.V., and other sexual transmitted diseases?

Everyone must take full responsibility for their own actions. So, you are part to blame for not making the correct choices in your life, and for rushing into things, such as this chapter describes.

If you don't look out for yourself, who else will? I am trying to, but it is up to you to open and receptive to the knowledge, wisdom and understanding given to you for you to... "RECOGNIZE GAME!"

Chapter Seven

THE EMPATHETIC &
SYMPATHETIC DECEPTION

I f you are unapprised on what is the true definition of the word empathy and sympathy, I will let you know here in a short moment. First, without expressing the knowledge you have in action, you might as well say that wisdom acquired was in vain, frivolous, and obsolete.

The two verbs described in this chapter are derivatives of love. Love unexpressed is not love at all. the word empathy means, the identification with and understanding the feelings of another person. The word sympathy means, Showing kindness, mutual understanding, or affection during a time of sadness or loss.

For example, you see an 85-year-old lady pushing a cart full of groceries across the parking lot towards her car. You see that she is totally uncomfortable and about a second from passing out, due to the scorching heat.

Here you are, straight out of an aerobics class, dressed in yoga pants and sneakers, carrying a 16-ounce V-8. You are headed in the same direction of the older woman. What are you going to do? Are you going to use your empathy and sympathy, or are you going to ignore your intuition?

Now, we both know that there is more to this story. That is why I deliberately left out the word, "DECEPTION" Using your empathy and sympathy for goodness sake is good, but when an individual, such as this guy, uses and twist this principal in a nefarious way, that is when it becomes wrong.

Showing love is supposed to be in a giving way, and only expecting "GOD" to reward you for your acts of kindness, charity, gentleness, and generosity. In prison, some convicts conjured up a phrase called, "The catch 22." It is used when they do someone a favor or give someone some sort of a gift. The "green" person accepts it as a gift, but later finds out the hard way that the gift wasn't actually a gift at all! The gift had some serious strings attached. More than likely, the "green" person wouldn't have accepted the gift if they knew previously that they would be charged an enormous amount of crazy interest in return.

This usually happens to the ones who has never been to prison before. Also, they may be scared.

This so-called player has the vision to spot women's inner most needs. He is very aware of the heartache, pain, and the ups and downs of life that most women go through. Really, who does not want someone to listen to them and to have someone's shoulder to lean on? Who isn't lonely and needs companionship? This conniving person makes it his duty to be there at your weakest point! Why? Because if there is only one thing that he will ever know for sure is, any person breathing in oxygen will always remember the person who was there for them when they needed them the most!

They are the most appreciative ones because if you weren't there to help, they could have spiraled down into the depths unknown. Naturally, deep down inside, they really want to do something nice for you and to be there for you in your time of need. Only a complete jerk, butthole, or a pure heifer wouldn't be.

This guy usually seems to have it all together. He has the persona, the clothes, cars, and the money. It is very difficult for him not to use his swagger. He just seems to be aware of everyone's struggle in life.

They are always with a crappy car, too many kids, and mothers without father's around.   There are too many people ogling and

THE EMPATHETIC & SYMPATHETIC DECEPTION

drooling at his swagger. He just seems to be aware of everyone struggles in life. They are all around him 24/7.

But that is exactly how he got to his newly found status! He was once poor and was determined to break out of the grips of poverty by adopting this motto, The rich get richer, while the poor get poorer. He deliberately adopted the bloodsucker poor slogan. In his mind, his thoughts are filled with, Better him than me. Better I than someone else. Sooner or later it was about to happen and no one's going to look out for me attitude. All day long it is me, myself, and I twirling around in his head.

There is no need prolonging your hunger anymore. I am going to give you a couple of vivid past experiences when I once used this deception...

The objectives name was Michell Black. She was 35 years old, pale white skin complexion, green eyes, and had shoulder length black hair.

It was one of those gorgeous sunny days outside and me and two of my male friends were entertaining three lovely ladies at their condo. We were drinking Hennessey and coke, experiencing with a little marijuana, playing cards and laughing about having fun at high noon on a Saturday.

There was one thing that I was not going to let happen, and that was to let the drinks run out. I knew my partners could drink, but these women weren't really women! They were 120-pound catfish! It wasn't 30 minutes before that 1/2 gallon turned into a damn shot glass!

I stood up and said, "Hey! I am fixing to go to the liquor store and by some more alcohol. I will be back in a few." One female said, "There is a liquor store just up the street. Do you need some money?" I looked at her like Yep! She is the one I am going to hook up with. She is the nice and thoughtful one.

I lied and told everyone that I have never been to this side of town before. So, I already knew about the liquor store up the street. It was connected to the college neighborhood 7/11, laundry mat, and a carwash. From sunup to sundown, that place was crawling with all types of women! Black, light skinned, high yellow, skinny, toned, thick, white, Indian, Asian, and Arab women everywhere! All these beautiful flavors of women ranging from 18-50 years old.

I was eager to leave that little get together. That is when I spotted two women as I pulled up and parked in front of the 7/11. They were getting out of a two-door blue neon. Both were wearing bright multicolored summer dresses. Naturally, I chose the driver to speak to.

After a few minutes of pleasant inquiries, the driver suggested that I bring a friend over to her place in 5 minutes! I thought to myself, 5 minutes? I shouldn't have lied to the girl and said that I was going to pick a friend up and hang out! Plus, I shouldn't have told her that I was fixing to buy a 1/2 gallon of Hennessy either! Oh well, I cannot leave these two fish on the hook. I might as well fry them.

I told Maria, (Michelle's friend) "Make it 10 minutes." She gave me the address and directions to the same condo we were already at! I went inside the store, bought the new party some cogna, and picked up some cheap Christian Brothers for the previous party. My intentions were to lie and say they ran out of Hennessey and grab one of my friends to come ride with me to go to another liquor store, but in all actuality, we were headed to the other side of the condominiums to entertain Maria and Michelle.

My plan was executed with precision. We walked up to the stairs and rang the doorbell. Maria answered and let us in. I introduced my friend, Marcus to them and we started mingling immediately. I am not going to sit here and lie to you. I picked, Maria because I thought she would be the easiest and quickest lay. An hour into the mini get together, Marcus and Michelle took off up the stairs. I am stuck downstairs trying to save face by remaining cool, but inside I am furious! I just left some 100% sure sex and a 90% chance of having a swinger session for this deceptive, penis teasing floozy? And to make matters worse, the friend I hooked Michelle up with (that is upstairs getting it on) is leaving the very next day for the military! Plus, she doesn't even know this.

I found out that I got played and Michelle will find out tomorrow.

A long strenuous and treacherous hour of small talk went on until the love birds came down looking like newlyweds. Maria said, "Aquarius, I would have given you some, but I know that you are just a player." Then Michelle said, "Yep! You can tell, I am glad I met Marcus!" I am sitting there stunned and utterly flabbergasted! Didn't they know that birds of a feather flock together? I thought to myself. Again, I thought, Oh, I see. I am too flashy, flamboyant, clean, and got too much money and pizzazz. Plus, I am the coach and owner of the player association. Deep down I wanted to blow up and expose it all, Marcus included, but due to friendship I kept silent.

Finally, we left and Marcus said, "Damn, dog them broads were stupid as hell! Old girl's vagina was good though. Too bad that she will never see me again. I am married anyways!" I simply nodded my head, dropped him off at the previous party where we left our other friend stranded, and I went to one of my girlfriend's house.

A week later, Michelle called me, she said, "Aquarius, have you heard from Marcus? he said he was going to call me the next day, but hasn't." Inside, I laughed. I totally had forgotten about both women and Marcus were probably having sex with some afghan chic by now. So, to make me feel good and to make her feel bad, I leaped at the opportunity to expose the truth. I said, "I am sorry, Michelle darling, but Marcus left to the military the next day, baby." There was dead silence on the other end and then, Michell said, "But he told me that he wanted to get a place together and that in a week or so he was supposed to meet with a real estate agent, concerning a house." I thought, Damn! Marcus sold her a big ass dream!

Next, I said, "Baby, I am sorry, but the true player played you. Plus, he is married." Then she went on to say, "But Aquarius, I gave my landlord my two weeks' notice and I will have to leave soon. Plus, he already has someone who has put down a deposit and paid the first month's rent." I thought, yet again, Daaaaaamn! Marcus sold her a fantastic dream and she bit for it big time!

On the other hand, was it my problem? I got clowned that day and I know they talked about me behind my back. So, I said, "I am sorry, baby." Michelle started crying. Next, she hung up the phone. Like I said before, sympathy and empathy met, but not put into action isn't sympathy and empathy at all.

Five days have gone by and Michelle called me again! She said, "Hi, Aquarius. What are you doing?" I am thinking, Girl, what is done is done. Stop calling me. So, I say, "Nothing. What's up?" Michelle said, "I found me another place and I was wondering if you could help me move?" What in the hell is the matter with this woman? She has a lot of nerves! She didn't have anyone else to call. Well, hell, I guess I would be nice, but she is going to have to give me some money! I say, "Look, you are going to have to buy me dinner or something." Michelle replied, "okay." Next, she gave me the directions to her place.

This girl worked the hell out of me! It took the entire day! After it was over with, Michelle said, "Aquarius, you are so sweet! Thank you for helping me. What would you like to eat?" I looked at her like, "BITCH! Are you serious? I am ready to get the fuck away from you!" Then I said, "I will have to decline, baby doll. You take care of yourself." Then I left.

The look on her face was somewhat a disappointing one, but I really didn't like being nice because I thought that was a sign of weakness.

Two weeks later, again this crazy bitch calls me! Michelle said, "Aquarius, I am sorry to bother you again. I am at work, and my car won't start. Could you come pick me up?" I said, "Alright, I will be there in 15 minutes."

You see, I understood a lot mainly due to my gift of empathizing and sympathizing, but this dame needed a man, bad! I started to feel like I was there being drugged into the position, but was receiving the relationship perks, like, intimacy, conversation, food, and sex!

When I pulled up to her job, she was standing amongst a clique of females. Studying their body language, she must have told all about me, but they thought it was too good to be true until I pulled up and got out of the car!

I went straight up to the chick clique of 5 women and shook all their hands (because I am a gentleman) and said, "I am Aquarius. How are all of you beautiful ladies doing? Michelle, you ready to go. I will have a tow truck come pick up your car." Yes, I put on a good show for her. That was right up my alley.

When she sat down in the passenger's seat, I said, "Look, I will pay for the hauling of your car, pay to get it fixed plus, I will come pick you up and take you to work until it gets fixed, okay?" She was shocked into silence! I almost killed her with kindness! Finally, she turned down my mind pounding music and said, "Aquarius, thank you. I appreciate everything you have done for me. You are not all that hard as you come off to be. You are really nice and sweet person." I cut the music back up and said, "Don't ever turn my music down again", in a jokingly yet serious manner.

After a week of being her taxicab, every day she asked to see if I wanted to come inside of her place. I always declined, due to the fact, I always had prior engagements. But this night, I didn't have any. Michelle was persistent. She said, "Aquarius, when are you going to come in and see my new place, damn!"

What she didn't know was that I didn't want to be told no about anything. Plus, I was seriously attracted to her and her voluptuous body. Also, I was really a serious player and I didn't want to take advantage of her because I knew what she has been through. Plus, she was extremely lonely and vulnerable. At the time, I was a good guy, but I wasn't going to be a fake one either.

So, I went into her place of residency. I looked around and told her that she arranged everything well. Next, I took a seat and she gave me a glass of Coke-a-Cola. The time was 10pm. It was sort of odd because to me, that is the beginning time for a booty call.

Then she said, "Aquarius, make yourself at home while I take a hot shower." I started feeling trapped! Then I watched her walk away from me. Those perfect gluten just a sashaying back and forth. Damn! I thought. I sure would like to have a serving of that! But nope, I need to cut off my lust vision and just chill.

Michelle came out 15 minutes later with her hair wet and wearing a white robe. My lustful thoughts zooming. She is totally naked underneath! Trying to control them, I thought, hell, it is her home and she just got off work. She is entitled to do as she pleases.

Then out of the blue, Michelle said, "Aquarius, will you come and lay down with me and just hold me?" That did it! I stood up and said, "I am sorry but that is something that I would do after I made love to a woman. I don't know what you are up to, but I am not up for the games, okay?" Then Michelle says, "Aquarius, I know but I am afraid that you will just do me like everyone else has done and leave me after you had sex with me."

Well, she had a point there. At least she was learning from her mistakes. So, I said, "If it's good, I will keep on coming back!"

You see, when you are sad, depressed, down, and out, and lonely, you are at your weakest point. It is easy for you to cloud your own judgement. You are automatically setting yourself up for failure to get manipulated by any type of individual.

So, consider being very careful in deciding who you confide in and ...RECOGNIZE GAME!

Chapter Eight

The Good Dad Illusion

Are you the type of woman that likes dogs or like to walk dogs? Well, if by any chance that you are, think of that feeling you get when you see a really cute dog in the park or cute puppy in the window. Do you say, "Oooh, he is soooo cute!" Then you wish that you had the finances and the time to purchase the dog and take him home.

It takes a lot of time, money and energy to take care of a newborn puppy. Many mothers can identify with this but having a puppy and raising a real human being is totally different.

This day in age, father's seen out and about with a newborn or a toddler is damn near extinct. Single fathers with a newborn or a toddler are rarely heard of. But wouldn't it be just adorable if you see a father toting around a precious and cute baby girl through the mall or grocery store while doing some shopping?

Of course, you would. You would look at that man and think, " That is so sweet! It is good to see a father taking care and spending time with his daughter. If you are a single mother, you would think, 1) My little girl's father is a piece of cow dung! 2) That is a good man right there. 3) I wish my I had him. As a matter of fact, he is kind of sexy taking care of his child

You know, that is a good thing, but some men aren't consciously aware that women of all ages and ethnic groups are staring at him. They are like the guy who loves his $5,000.00 pit bull and honestly loves taking him out for a walk in the park.

After a while, the formerly unconscious father is suddenly transformed by the overwhelming attention of women. All the, "excuse me, what is her name" and all of the "Oh! She is so cute." And how old is she," etc... has slowly but surely turned him out.

Now, in his mind, he is thinking, Hell, this is a good way to meet women. Besides my daughters' mother was a complete bitch. What started out so simple and pure, due to the cards that life dealt, turned into a means of getting your attention.

Really, wouldn't you think that single dads and mothers would have something in common anyways? Well, if you value my advice, if they merge their lives will become easier. They would be no longer single and could take turns staying home with the children, cooking, sex, and splitting the bills 50/50. That is if the "good dad" really wanted to.

On the other hand, what does the single dad have in common with a single lady without children? Well, if this woman is looking and doesn't mind him having a child who he solely takes care of, this guy, to her, would be the perfect catch. The situation would not seem like a risk to her. She would already have all the data she needs. He has a job, good looking, caring, stable, and responsible. Plus, he is mature and a good dad! She would know that his nights would be at home too. So, all she must do is fit into his schedule.

This person and any female interested in him would see eye to eye. They would have a silent, mutual, unspoken understanding, the child comes first. So, if he needs to get off the phone, end a date early, neglect you for weeks at a hand, or keep you from coming to his house because the uncertainty of you being around for the long haul, and breaking his kids heart. There would be no arguing because you would understand!

Ha! You may have been a victim of the illusion. He could have had another person to go out with or to come over to his place that you have never seen before. Just like the single mothers, they always find a way to get away!

This guy has so much game and a lot of money. Plus, he has a huge load of family and friends who would be more than happy to take their grandchild, daughter, or niece for a couple of hours a night or even a weekend.

If not, I guarantee you that he has multiple babysitters on call. Plus, he will only work 5 to 6 days a week, tops! This player can sleep with a lot of women in an 8 hours' time frame easily! Take me at my word. I promise you; I have done it all!

Then you have the uncles and frustrated friends perpetrating as a father. They took the kid to get an ice cream while "the good dad" made a quick errand to pay a bill or something of that nature. You saw him, approached him, and complimented the baby. Then, he said, "Yep! I am a proud single dad. His or her mom took off with another guy." Bam! You are hooked believing the lie. The two of you exchange information, and the game has just begun.

Then you have the type that admit they have children and they take care of them just so you wouldn't think that they were a deadbeat dad, but really aren't doing a damn thing for their child.

It is crazy, huh? Well, it is true. There is also a different twist to the good dad illusion. It is where a single guy gets in with a single mother's kids and deliberately shows kindness, love, and affection to her kids just so she could see that he is "God" with her kids. Especially, when the kids show a likeness toward him and always asking of him.

Personally, I have never used this technique, but have had several occurrences where I could have used it. To me as long as I knew that I was doing what I was supposed to do, concerning the responsibilities of my children, I could not of cared less what any woman thought. I felt like I had way too much game to stoop down to this level, but I will tell you a story of a "reversed good dad illusion" that stems off the main idea of this subject.

One evening at a nightclub, I was standing at the entrance and exit from the dance floor. I am sort of tipsy and just standing there being observant of my surroundings. I have a weird fetish for feet and stilettos on the feet. Somewhere down the line, I brainwashed myself into thinking that you could know a lot about a woman by examining her feet and the type of shoes she wears. I am not into licking toe jam and any weird sexual fantasies of that nature, but I do appreciate a good, soft, and well pedicured feet.

So, I am standing here astonished and bewildered by these big ass soldiers stiletto boots! I am trying to get a description of what type of woman this is. As I finally came up with the idea that this lady is flamboyant, different, and super aggressive, I noticed the shoes heading my way.

They were getting closer and closer. I see all the feet bunched up together, So I look down at my own feet. I just bought some new Kenneth Cole shoes. (I cannot stand when someone's steps on my feet!) So, I am seeing "Jaws" coming and I think to myself, those shoes would hurt like hell if they stepped on my feet! Every step this woman took toward me, I felt myself getting in a defensive position.

As soon as the feet got within arm's length, I stuck out my arm and stiff armed the woman, and said, "If those clod hoppers step on my feet, I am going to be mad as fuck!" Then I rose my head up and looked her dead in her green eyes.

She looked down at her feet, glanced at mine, and laughed hard, and said, "What's your name?" I told her my name, what I did for a living (sort of), where I stayed (sort of), and what kind of car I drove.

Out of the blue, she asked, "Do you have any kids?" To her, I already knew that I was the perfect catch, but when she asked that question, telling her the truth could have pushed away my perfect catch! I wasn't going to tell her that I had 8 kids by 6 different women. So, I lied and said, "Nope! Maybe when I get around to it I might."

You see, these days, you cannot be naive and gullible. It may look good and seem good, but it isn't always as it seems. There are some professional magicians out there that can make you believe your panties are red, knowing damn well that you aren't even wearing any! So, my dear wise friend, don't go for the okie doke and... RECOGNIZE GAME!

Chapter Nine

THE TWO HUMAN CONSPIRACY

You have either heard about or have seen all the movies describing these characters, "Thelma & Louise, Bonnie & Clyde, Batman & Robin, Scarface & Manolo." Besides Batman and Robin, the other couples were together to plan a wrongful act in secret or worked together to do an evil act.

Each pair of individuals identify with the need for the other. They have the ability and foresight to see the strength in the other that compensates their weakness. This is a two-part version of Voltron, or it could remind you of the pimp and the prostitute, the boss and the secretary, or just summing it all up with the employer and the employee.

If you take one of them away, there wouldn't have been any movies, no hero, no back robbery, no paperwork, no drug deal, or any type of legal or illegal businesses at all. They both would have been what I like to call, lost in the sauce. Together, they unite into a synergistic merger! They are both energy suckers. They get the adrenaline rush from feeding from the other. They are aware that there are powers with numbers, and smart enough to do the common denominational mathematics and eliminate the unnecessary numbers.

In the same sense, my friend, these two chaps (guys) have come together to conspire against you! More than likely, you will rarely meet them both from the beginning. There is always the leader, who goes out to case out (get information) or target (you!),

Whether his hidden intentions, are to marry you, have sex with you, to meet your friend, get you to trust him, burglarize your home, or rob your job, he will reach his objectives. The two conjured up a win/win outlook. It is the good cop/bad cop, bad cop/bad cop, and the good cop/good cop method. (Sort of speak) They are a team. It doesn't matter who go you because the profits are split 50/50 anyways.

Now, where there is love concerned, the payments turn into favors. I played this role for you, now it is your turn to return the favor. It is so crazy because you are the co-star in a major motion picture that is getting some serious game ran on, and you do not even know it! I have to admit, it is sort of unfair because while you are at home or at work, those two, they already know your lines, and they will even role play as your character! They are so proactive that they automatically know how you are going to react before you do!

There are so many twists to this conspiracy that it is pathetic. There are many meticulous and pathological extremities involved that it racks my brain just retrieving all the mendacious hoaxes. I will try to describe a few before I go into a small low budget movie.

Let's see, you have the, 1) Let's see if she is a two-faced tactic. 2) Long or short-term vision. 3) The adventurer risk taker. 4) What would she do for money tactics. 5) The how much will she run her mouth tactic.

Now, finally, are you ready for the final, past, personal experience of my life, so you can get a clearer and more in-depth insight into how and what effects and outcomes this conspiracy produces? Okay, fasten your seatbelt...

In this incident, I was silent co-conspirator unaware of being part of a plot that was ran on one of my fraudulent friends. The star lead was played by this conniving, scandalous, and devious Asian chic named, Zing Yao. She was the girlfriend of my fake friend named, Cain.

Me and Cain executed our game on several hundred women on

end. We would have a monthly competition on who could have sex with different women the most. Not that either one of us would lie because our track record spoke for itself. So, we came up with an idea to bring each lady to our town house to be shown as a "point." By the end of the year, I would be 10-1-1 or 9-2-1 (wins, losses, and ties) My highest score was 15 and my lowest was 8. My total average for the year was 12 a month.

So, one day I am chilling at our bachelor pad, taking a break from whoremongering, Cain walks in the door with this super bad (fine) Asian chic! (The finer they were, the better.) Immediately, I think, damn! he might want to consider giving up the player-ism for her because she is the best, he has ever caught all year long!

Cain walked by me and said, "What up, Playa? this is Zing." He had that smirk on his face and that look in his eye like he knew for sure he out done me this time. Instantly, I take a mental survey of all my "super bad" chicks and came up with several who was on Zings level and couple who were beyond her level. So being the C.E.O. of the "Players Klique Club," I brushed them both off.

One thing was certain, unless one of us pushed the female away, none of the 15-20 women were going anywhere.

The town house was the headquarters. There were 3 members and 10-15 trainees that would periodically stop by to get a whiff of some good games. The 3 members had at least "one" main girl amongst the bunch that they would go over their house and do the whole relationship thing. Sometimes, all 3 of us and our 3 lady friends would get together and go out on the town.

That is where it began to be a little dangerous for all of us. You have 3 attractive men with 3 different types of game, and 3 different types of women being exposed to it. Everyone's looking and studying everyone! But who will be the scandalous one to cross the line and stab the other in the back first?

I am over at my #2 main girls house. Something in my gut is telling me that something just isn't right. I cared for Kylie, but then again, I didn't. The code amongst us was, "Never to sleep with each other's woman." So, I used to let some of the fellas come hang out at her house.

Kylie was acting awkward. She seemed nervous and was being too nice toward me. This was weird because she was always mad at me, due to the fact, she knows I was cheating on her with other women. Mainly, because I would be talking to them sexually over the phone in front of her. Oh well, I thought. I was about ready to fire her anyways.

One of my trainees I named Silk called me and asked if he could come hang out. I said, "Yes, come over to Kylie's." He showed up 15 minutes later. When Kylie seen him (In hindsight) she took off to her bedroom. I didn't pay her any mind.

The next thing you know, Silk got awfully close to me and said, "Say, Aquarius, keep what I am fixing to say on the incognito, OK?" I turn my head to the left so I could look him directly in the eyes. After sensing that he was serious, I repositioned myself so I could relax while I receive the news. Next, I replied, "yes man. Go ahead and hit me off with it."

Silk leaned in a little closer, as if he were wearing Arrid extra dry and said, "Say man, last night, me and Cain stopped by here looking for you and Kylie let us in. I sat here on the couch while Cain went to the back and knocked off, Kylie." I said, "WHAT?" Silk said, "Cain slept with Kylie last night while you were gone, homie. I just felt like you should know because that wasn't right."

My heart turned into a hemi engine. It was revved up! I was furious! My best friend and my girlfriend conspired against me behind my back. Plus, I had to hear it from someone else other than one of them? I was hurt, but not wounded. Basically, I felt more betrayed than anything else.

Later, I confronted them both separately. Would you believe that they tried to sell me the exact, same story? Kylie said, "I am sorry, baby, but I was crying because you walked out on me. It just happened, and after 5 seconds I stopped him because it didn't feel right."

Cain said, "Ah man, it wasn't like that. We came looking for you and I saw Kylie crying. I was just checking to see if she was, OK. The next thing you know we ended up doing it for 5 seconds. I stopped and told her that I can't do this to my best friend."

I made them think that I was buying it, but who starts intercourse and doesn't finish it? Plus Cain was a male whore, and I made Kylie into a nympho, due to the fact, we would have sex 3 times a day. At least 45 minutes setting for a stretch of 1 1/2 years! Recently, for the last few weeks, I stopped having sex with her because she was making me mad.

After, Kylie and I broke up, a couple of months passed by and I get a call at my #1 girlfriends house, her name was Kay. On the other end of the line was Silk, Que, and Zing. They were telling me that, Cain got locked up.

Every time an emergency came up and it required knowledge and money, and I was sought out diligently.

The jail incident occurred frequently between us and the trainees, mainly due to a suspended license, no license, unpaid traffic ticket, or driving without insurance verification. I don't know what it was, but the entire crew didn't respect the traffic laws until they ended up in jail.

So, they are telling me that they just got off the phone with Cain and he has already told them how much his bond was and how abouts to get him out. Then, I said, "Why in the hell are you all calling me then? Cain don't need me. Zing, you got his money, don't you? He is telling you all the truth and all you are doing is wasting time." Then Zing said, "Well, I just need to make sure, that's all."

It was 7:30 am and my fake girl, Kay, had to be at work at 8 am. Usually, I would give her some "Have a great day," sex. Kay would take a shower and I would take her to work. Dealing with this situation had disturbed the morning routine and I was looking forward to that.

Next, I said, "Look, Zing! Everything is cool, but I must let you go. I must take Kay to work, but I will be back in 15 minutes. After you go bond out Cain, tell him to stop by." Zing said, "Okay."

Kay is walking around the house naked (the indicator). Then the phone rang again! This time it is Cain. I am thinking, DAMN! DAMN! DAMN! I have this fine, dark tanned, red hair, blue eyed, 5 ft 9-inch, 145-pound, naked woman praying around begging me to give it to her, I am being distracted!

Immediately, I said, "Hey man, your girl and a few of the boys just called me. Zing is on the way." Cain screams, "What!!!? I spoke to them 3 hours ago!" To myself, I thought, Damn, that is messed up. Then I said, "Don't worry about it. It's handled. I also told Zing that when you get out, to stop by here because I know that you are going to need some smoke." Cain replied, "Alright." Then we hung up.

Seeing that the time is 7:50 am, I located Kay in the bathroom fully dressed, placing her makeup on. I walk up behind her, hugged her from behind, and whispered, "I am so sorry baby. I know that you were looking forward to, have a great day, sex. I will make it up to you after you get off work."

On the way taking Kay to work, I explained to her the ordeal. She really didn't care and neither did I. I just didn't want her to think that something else was more important than her.

When we pulled up to her job, we kissed and said our I'll miss you, I'll be thinking of you, and I love you. Kay turned to get out of the car, and I smacked her left buttocks hard! (She like surprises, but it was mainly to give her something to look forward to) Kay jumped, turned around, smiled and said, 'You can't be doing that here! Everyone inside probably seen us!" Then I said, "That is why I did it, baby, so they could be jealous of you with their lonely butt. Finally, I drove off and headed back to her place to relax a bit and prep our dinner.

I arrived back at Kay's house at 8:10 am. I am feeling mentally drained. My intentions were to do a little spring cleaning, ironing, and relax. As soon as I walked through the door and saw that cozy and comfortable couch, all I could think about was sleeping. I had until 4 pm. What the rush? I thought. So, I ran straight toward the sofa like N.F.L. player does when diving into the end zone.

There was this loud ringing noise that startled me and ruined my sleep. It was the doorbell. I turn over and check the time. It said 9 am! Quickly, I thought, who the hell is this? No one comes over here without prior notification.

Shaking my head in total frustration, I begin walking toward the door, and I looked through the peephole and didn't see anyone. I opened the door, peeked my head out the door, and looked to the right, and standing there like a hooker in a dark, secluded alley was, Zing!

She was a petite Asian woman. She stood 5 ft all. She weighed around 100 pounds. Noticing her appearance, she was wearing more makeup than usual. Her hair was long, and it hung down to her bra strap.

This day her usual black straight hair was curly. Plus, she had on some 4 1/2-inch stilettos, a red tight halter top, and a short black mini skirt.

Looking at her puzzled, I said, "Zing, what's up? Where is Cain?" She replied, "I was on my way to bail him out." Somewhat bewildered, I saw that I was being rude, so I let her inside.

She walked past me slow with her eyebrows raised, looking suspicious and curious as if she wondered if we were alone or something. You see, Zing has seen me with all sorts of different women. She was around the crew so much that she was almost considered a part of the motherfucking crew! There were times when I used to tell Cain, "Hey man, I know this is your main squeeze and all, but all the women I bring here is starting to wonder if this is her place." Plus, I felt like I was being a buster by exposing my "player-ism" in front of a woman. Furthermore, I didn't even like Zing. I just respected her because she was my guy's woman.

After I closed the door, by this time my mind is racing, trying to make sense of what's really transpiring, and pissed off from all the days disruptions, twists, turns, disappointments, surprises, and mysteries. I sat down on the sofa, and said, "Zing, what are you doing here?" Still standing in the middle of the living room, looking everywhere, but at me, twirling her keys in her hand, she said, "I just thought I would stop by."

Finally, it clicked, my naive and gullible thoughts went ice cold! The player detectors, scanners and radars were beeping uncontrollably in my brain. Next, I said, "Oh! I know why you came over! You think that you are slick! Your boyfriend is in jail and since he cannot handcuff you, you are roaming free." (laughing all the while) "Plus, you knew that I was going to be here at Kay's place all alone. So, you thought you would come and see if I would be willing to play along, hey?"

Now, looking directly into my eyes, piercing through my soul, Zing said, "What makes you think something like that?" Tired of playing games, I said, "Look, Zing, if you want to have some fantastic, mind blowing sex, you need to hurry up because my homeboy is waiting for you."

In my mind, I am sitting there shaking my head, thinking during this entire time that she has been with my friend, she has been waiting patiently for the opportunity to sleep with me. Then Zing said, "You think that you know everything, don't you?" Next, I rose up from the sofa and approached Zing. Simultaneously, unbuttoning my shirt. I got within a nose length away from her nose, grabbed her hand and placed it on my naked chest.

When her other hand came up to rub all over me, I knew that the deal was sealed. In my mind, I am thinking, two wrongs don't make a right, so I am going to turn left! Filled with overwhelming fleshly lust, we ferociously and hungrily kissed each other with so much passion, Zing stopped me and said, "Aquarius, I want you to treat me like a dirty whore ass slut and fuck the shit out of me doggy style on Kay's bed!"

Back then, I knew how to read in between the lines and could take a hint. So, if a person suggests that was directly up my alley, they sure as heck didn't have to tell me twice! I swooped Zing up in my arms like a newlywed husband does his newly wed wife and carried her through the threshold in order to fulfill her request.

You see in this particular case; the leader was a female conspiring with me against her boyfriend. It is self-evident on what type of payment she was looking for, but just think if it was you who were in Cain's shoes. How would you feel? Keep your seatbelt fastened because the next illustration is derived from the same characters, but has different conspiracy paradigm...

You are aware that even though me and Zing conspired against, Cain, we automatically conspired against Kay while she was at work, also.

Noon rolls around and I just happened to look out the window when I spotted Zings car pull back up. This time she had Cain in the passenger's seat. From the looks of it, it seemed like he is fresh out of jail.

I opened the front door and retrieved to the Lazy boy recliner, thinking Damn! I have the slightest clue how this is going to transpire. I know he is mad as hell for being locked up 9 hours when it only takes an hour. Plus, I just got done banging his #1 girls brains out. She must smell like sex! I wonder if he senses any foul play.

Interrupting my thoughts, they both stroll through the door holding hands! I am thinking to myself, this scandalous bitch! I bet you a million bucks to a dime that she kissed him, too! Knowing that she didn't change panties, shower, gargle, or brush her teeth!

Cain's red Boston red socks hat was cocked to the side like he was some type of gangster or something. (I have seen it so many times where people "act" all hard when they get out of prison, or jail), but all he did was 9 hours at a college town jail. His usual, happy to see Aquarius smile was nowhere to be found, and by the looks of it, he seemed to be pulling Zing along instead of calmly strolling along. He had this, Super Macho aria illuminating from him, saying, 'yeah, this is my bitch! No one in the galaxy can have her.' type of attitude. Deep down inside, I was laughing pretty damn hard.

Zing is looking like she just finished 1st in the 200-meter hurdles. Then she said, "Hi, Aquarius. Where is Kay?" I hated being in this treacherous, deceptive, Benedict Arnold, secret keeping position, but I played along with her and said, "She is at work. I am going to pick her up at around 4 pm."

Next, I turn my attention to Cain standing there looking like he is giving us both the benefit of the doubt, but not really and said, "What is up dawg?" Next, I told him, "Have a seat and roll up one for us... I know that you need it." Then I tossed him a sandwich bag full of cookie flower. The smile returned and all doubts were erased from his mind for that second.

Forty-five minutes and seven Zigzags later, the three of us are sitting there in a room full of smoke! Everyone's eyes are bloodshot! The two "lovebirds" are nestled together like there isn't a worry in the world.

Not knowing if it is the narcotics playing with my hearing or what, I could have sworn I heard some keys in the door a second ago. Suddenly, Kay comes bursting through the door. Immediately, I got a 95% sober. Not because of my company, or the smoke lingering in the air, but it was the guilt and shame that was being held inside, eating me alive.

Honestly, I don't know how people do it! I cannot hold my water, but I can hold someone else's. It's better for me to avoid putting myself in difficult situations because I will tell on my damn self!

Kay walked straight over to me and sat in my lap and gave me a hug and a kiss. I am thinking, I am just as scandalous as, Zing, but at least I took a shower and brushed my teeth! Next, Kay said, "I am so glad they let me off work early. Now, we can spend the day together." I thought, if it was any earlier, someone would have been dead.

Zing shifts around in her seat and said, "Hi, Kay. I love those shoes that you are wearing." I am wondering how many times Zing has done this type of thing. For me, she was way too calm. Secondly, it seemed that being close and personal to the victims doesn't faze her one bit! Last, but not the least, she is so good of an actress that I am mulling it over in my head contemplating if the nefarious sex act even took place!

Sensing that Kay wanted some quality time alone with me, I told my company they had to go. Simple and plain and just like that.

A few days past and by the grace of God, I caught up on some rest and chores without any drama. So, I decided to go visit one of my only platonic, lady friends. (Mentioned in chapter 4.) As soon as I walked through the door, I saw a trainee and Mag, the other playa partner, sitting in the living room listening to music. Usually, I would have said hi to May and left because if I wanted to see some fellas, I knew where the headquarters was located. Since I haven't seen Mag in a week or so, I decided to stay.

Sporadically me and Zings mendacious activity convicted me of guilt and condemnation. So, I saw Mag as an opportunity to vent. I sat down on his right side, turned my head to the left and said, "Say, playa, I have some news that will give someone the blues!" Mag said, "Cut it out. Are you serious? Tell me what is up, Playa!"

I ran down the situation to him as vividly as possible. His mouth stood gaped open during the whole time I was giving him the details. After I was done, he said, "Damn! I wouldn't of thought Zing was like that in a thousand years! She is an undercover freak!" Then he said, "Look here Aquarius, see if you can get her to come and swing (have a threesome) with the both of us." I said, "Hell nah, man! I still have to let Cain know what type of girl he is in love with." Mag replied, "He is not going to like that, but before you do that, you might as well see if she will swing one! I bet you she has thought about it."

Somewhat convinced, I thought, well he has a point to a degree, and it has been a while since me and the fellas swung one. Oddly no one knew her phone number. Next, Mag said, "May just got off the phone with her because she called to see if Cain was here. May said no but invited her over. And Zing said that she was on the way." That made up my mind. We were going to test my game. I saw it as a personal challenge to see if I could whodini Zing into a threesome and expose her to another member and friend of the Klique.

Twenty minutes past by and May had to go make a run. The trainee had to leave. Now, it is just me and Mag sitting there waiting for, Zing. I spoke up and said, "Look, Mag. You let me do all of the talking, and when I say something just agree, okay?" Mag said, "You know I am down with it."

We see Zing's car pull up in May's driveway. I motion for Mag to sit at the far end of the sofa while I got the door. The doorbell rang. I deliberately counted to 10 before answering the door, had to make it seem like we were busy. Opening up the door, I immediately transform into acting role of shock and surprise and said," What's up, Zing? what are you doing here? Come on in. May had to make a run somewhere. I don't know when she will be back." Zing replied, "Oh, well can I come in and wait?"

Bam! She was busted! This chic was an opportunist! At this point in time, it wouldn't have mattered if we accidentally bumped into each other coming and going from a gas station restroom! As long as we were both alone, she was willing and able. What Zing didn't know we that we weren't alone. Plus, she was unaware that she was being conspired against this time.

Looking at me while licking her lips while walking past me, her body language suggested that we hurry up and make it quick! Between her third and fourth step past me, she stopped and grabbed her chest. She was startled by the sight of Mag and said, "You scared me! I didn't think there was anyone else in the house. How are you doing, Mag?" Mag, playing the dumb role said, "Fine, just chilling." I am looking at the scene as if on a balcony, and thought, good boy! The less you say, the greater chance we have on pulling this off.

Just like I anticipated, Zing took a seat smack dead in the middle of the sofa. If she sat at the end, it wouldn't have looked right. It would look suspicious of her. So, I sat on the far opposite end of the extremely long couch; therefore, if someone did stop by, Zing would look comfortable and respected. Plus, I didn't want to blow her cover, just yet, in front of Mag.

Suddenly, the phone rang. I answered it. It was May. She said that she was going to go out with one of her girlfriends and for me to lock up whenever I left. I spoke really loudly. Repeating what may had said so that Zing could hear that there would be no disturbances. Plus, to see if she would stick around or not.

Sensing that Zing grabbed my hint. I saw the tension leave her body as she readjusted herself and kicked her tennis shoes off, exposing her pedicured feet. she was still looking a bit awkward since three is a crowd. I did have the power to make Mag leave and Zing knew it, but my words had already left my mouth and went into the atmosphere.

Mag was surprising me. His mouth stayed shut. Prior to this situation, out of anger, I told Mag that I would never hook him up with another one of my girls. All because he didn't know how to be an Indian. Some people desperately want to be a chief, but don't have the chief's understanding. In other words, when out of position, the chemistry is out of balance, they mess up everything!

Witnessing that he is fully aware of this chance to redeem himself and get back in good rapport with me, I walk over and sat extremely close to Zing. Her eyes got big, and she stole a quick glance at Mag out of the corner of her eyes. Nervousness and embarrassment radiated all around her as she tucked her hair behind her left ear. Deep down inside, I was loving the fact that, Zing was feeling uneasy. So, I pressed onward.

I reached over and rubbed her thigh and slightly licked the outer surface of her ear lobe. Next, I said, "baby, we have about 30 minutes to get it on and don't pay any attention to Mag over there, okay?"

Zing leaned away from me, put her hand on mine to stop the thigh caressing, and looks at me like, what the hell? Are you crazy? So, I said, "Okay, that's how you going to act? Well, I already told Mag how I had your head rammed in Kay's headboard while Cain was waiting for his number one girl to come and bail him out."

I never seen a dark-skinned Asian turn white so quickly. Zings mouth dropped open so wide that you could have stuck a football inside of it! Now, that she was exposed, she got even more uncomfortable. She took off her jacket, put a leg underneath her buttocks, leaned back, crossed her arms and pierced a death look into my eyes.

Next, I said, "as a matter of fact, I bet you have been wanting to sleep with Mag secretly, too! Well, here is your chance, baby. Let's have a threesome. It'll be our secret and we won't tell, Cain."

I motioned Mag to come a little closer and asked for his terms of agreement. He obliged, and said, "yes, Zing no one will find out. I promise." Zing was turned on by the thought of being scandalous and sleeping with the both of us. Next, she said, "Are you sure that May or Cain won't pop up on us? Promise that you won't tell Cain?" Like two contestants at a family feud waiting for the host to finish his questions, we both said, "Yes!"

My dear lady friend, in any aspect of life, you may have to conspire with someone in order to reach your objective. Just be aware that the "conspirator" could easily be the "conspirer."

All humans have some sort of vulnerability. It may not be like Zings, but eager to exploit and manipulate any area that you love, so, if I were you, I would consider being cautious and aware of your surroundings, friends, associates, coworkers, and even family. Most importantly, seek discernment, and .... RECOGNIZE GAME!

Epilogue

My dear friend, out of the nine chapters previously described, I am more than positive that you have either been a victim of a few techniques or would like to. (Without the game playing, of course.) By any chance, that you were "played," I would like to offer you my condolences. On the other hand, if you would like for a guy to sincerely treat you like the unique and elegant queen that you are, this is perfectly natural.

This book was not written to deter or confirm your derogatory beliefs on finding true love. As a matter of fact, this manual was written for your admonition. Also, it was composed to give you a sense of discernment in order to correctly make the profitable investments of your only currency... TIME.

There are a lot of good, single, and hurt meant out there with emotional baggage, that is hiding behind a wall in order to protect themselves from the same fears you contain. If you are willing to chisel through that wall, I will guarantee you that would be worth the sacrifice, in order to achieve your desired result. If you are unwilling to, then I guarantee you a lifelong process of hurt, pain, and loneliness.

Why? Because a wise man or woman will test before they trust. They are mature and aren't easily foiled. Let's be practical for a moment. Would you buy a home without looking throughout the entire house or calculating the cost? Well, would you sign a contract without reading it? If you are the type of person that easily trust, hopefully this book has illuminated and awakened your senses.

Please allow me to ask you a question, "who is really responsible?" Is it the seller or the buyer? If you value my advice, the seller cannot force you into buying anything he is selling. Yes, he could be the best liar in the galaxy and try his damnedest to make you think that that Hyundai is really a Honda, but if you do the proper and necessary research, investigating into what he is selling, you will be able to see for yourself if it is the truth or not.

I say that to mention this, everyone walking the face of this earth is responsible for their own actions and decisions. Sometimes the truth is hard to swallow, but once swallowed it sets well in our gut.

I really hope that your present decision making will bring you everlasting joy. Consider not letting those past dead beats, suckers, and fears keep you from reaching and searching for that special one that our Creator intended for you to be with. I love you and take excellent care of yourself.

Sincerely,

Your friend,

—Aquarius

www.ingramcontent.com/pod-product-compliance
Lightning Source LLC
Chambersburg PA
CBHW050545280326
41933CB00011B/1730